THE PRACTICAL STEP-BY-STEP GUIDE TO
BAKING BREAD

THE PRACTICAL STEP-BY-STEP GUIDE TO
BAKING BREAD

70 FOOLPROOF RECIPES FOR CLASSIC BREADS, SHOWN IN 350 PHOTOGRAPHS

HOW TO BAKE AUTHENTIC ARTISAN LOAVES FROM ALL AROUND THE WORLD

CHRISTINE INGRAM AND JENNIE SHAPTER

southwater

This edition is published by Southwater, an imprint of Anness Publishing Ltd, Blaby Road, Wigston, Leicestershire LE18 4SE; info@anness.com

www.southwaterbooks.com; www.annesspublishing.com

If you like the images in this book and would like to investigate using them for publishing, promotions or advertising, please visit www.practicalpictures.com for more information.

Publisher: Joanna Lorenz
Project Editors: Linda Fraser and
    Kate Eddison
Copy Editors: Janet Charatan,
Jo Lethaby and Jenni Fleetwood
Designer: Nigel Partridge
Photographers: Nick Dowey (recipes)
    and Amanda Heywood
Home Economists: Jennie Shapter
    (recipes) and Jill Jones
Production Controller: Wendy Lawson

ETHICAL TRADING POLICY
At Anness Publishing we believe that business should be conducted in an ethical and ecologically sustainable way, with respect for the environment and a proper regard to the replacement of the natural resources we employ. As a publisher, we use a lot of wood pulp to make high-quality paper for printing, and that wood commonly comes from spruce trees.
We are therefore currently growing more than 750,000 trees in three Scottish forest plantations: Berrymoss (130 hectares/320 acres), West Touxhill (125 hectares/305 acres) and Deveron Forest (75 hectares/185 acres). The forests we manage contain more than 3.5 times the number of trees employed each year in making paper for the books we manufacture.

Because of this ongoing ecological investment programme, you, as our customer, can have the pleasure and reassurance of knowing that a tree is being cultivated on your behalf to naturally replace the materials used to make the book you are holding.

Our forestry programme is run in accordance with the UK Woodland Assurance Scheme (UKWAS) and will be certified by the internationally recognized Forest Stewardship Council (FSC). The FSC is a non-government organization dedicated to promoting responsible management of the world's forests. Certification ensures forests are managed in an environmentally sustainable and socially responsible way. For further information about this scheme, go to www.annesspublishing.com/trees

A CIP catalogue record for this book is available from the British Library.

Previously published as
Bread Baker's Bible

NOTES
Bracketed terms are intended for American readers.

For all recipes, quantities are given in both metric and imperial measures and, where appropriate, in standard cups and spoons. Follow one set of measures, but not a mixture, because they are not interchangeable.

Standard spoon and cup measures are level. 1 tsp = 5ml, 1 tbsp = 15ml, 1 cup = 250ml/8fl oz.

Australian standard tablespoons are 20ml. Australian readers should use 3 tsp in place of 1 tbsp for measuring small quantities.

American pints are 16fl oz/2 cups. American readers should use 20fl oz/2.5 cups in place of 1 pint when measuring liquids.

Electric oven temperatures in this book are for conventional ovens. When using a fan oven, the temperature will probably need to be reduced by about 10–20°C/20–40°F. Since ovens vary, you should check with your manufacturer's instruction book for guidance.

The nutritional analysis given for each recipe is calculated per portion (i.e. serving or item), unless otherwise stated. If the recipe gives a range, such as Serves 4–6, then the nutritional analysis will be for the smaller portion size, i.e. 6 servings. The analysis does not include optional ingredients, such as salt added to taste.

Medium (US large) eggs are used unless otherwise stated.

Main front cover image shows Pain Bouillie – for recipe, see page 58.

PUBLISHER'S NOTE
Although the advice and information in this book are believed to be accurate and true at the time of going to press, neither the authors nor the publisher can accept any legal responsibility or liability for any errors or omissions that may have been made nor for any inaccuracies nor for any loss, harm or injury that comes about from following instructions or advice in this book.

CONTENTS

INTRODUCTION

There is something undeniably special about bread. The flavour of a good loaf, the texture of the soft crumb contrasting with the crispness of the crust, is almost a sensual experience. Who can walk home with a fresh baguette without slowly, almost absent-mindedly breaking off pieces to eat en route? Or resist the promise of a slice of a soft white farmhouse loaf, spread simply with butter? Most people have their own favourite: ciabatta, rich with olive oil; dark, malty rye; honeyed *challah* or a Middle Eastern bread, freshly baked and redolent of herbs and spices. Whatever the shape or texture, bread has a special place in our affections.

Even today, at the start of the 21st century, when bread is taken largely for granted, seen as an accompaniment or a "carrier" for other foods, we still have a sense of its supreme significance. In some languages the word "bread" means "food", and in certain of the more rural parts of Spain and Italy, for example, you may find that bread is blessed or kissed before being broken or eaten. There are numerous rituals and traditions attached to bread. Slashing the dough with a cross or making a sign of the Cross over the loaf before baking was believed to let the devil out. Cutting the bread at both ends was also recommended to rid the house of the devil. One extraordinary custom was

ABOVE: Just a few of the many shapes and types of bread.

sin-eating, a practice at funerals, whereby someone would eat a loaf of bread and by so doing would take on the sins of the dead person.

The obvious explanation for bread's importance is that until quite recently, it was for many, quite literally the "staff of life" – the single essential food. Today, most people have more varied diets. Potatoes, pasta and rice are all enjoyed in the West and are important staple foods, but in some countries, for example France and Italy, bread is easily the most popular of the carbohydrates, eaten with every meal and in many cases with every course.

Like wine tasters, true aficionados taste bread *au naturel* in order to savour its unique taste and texture, unadulterated by other flavours. Good as this can be, the best thing about bread is that it goes so well with other foods. Throughout Europe bread is most frequently cut or broken into pieces to be eaten with a meal – to mop up soups and sauces or to eat with hams, pâtés and cheese. Dark rye breads, spread with strongly flavoured cheese or topped with smoked fish, are popular in northern Europe, and in the Middle East breads are split and stuffed with meats and salads – a tradition that has been warmly embraced in the West too. In

Britain and the USA, the European custom of serving bread with a meal, with or instead of potatoes or rice, is catching on, but sandwiches are probably still the favourite way of enjoying bread. Sandwiches have been going strong for a couple of hundred years – invented, it is said, by John Montagu, 4th Earl of Sandwich, so that he could eat a meal without having to leave the gaming table. Although baguettes and bagels are naturally ideally suited for linking bread with meat, the sandwich, clearly an English concept, is unique and continues to be the perfect vehicle for fillings that become more and more adventurous.

BREADS OF TODAY

Figures show that throughout Europe bread consumption declined after World War II. Until then it was the single most important food in the diet, but due to increased prosperity, which meant a wider choice of other foods, and mass production, which led to bread becoming increasingly insipid and tasteless, people moved away from their "daily bread". The situation was more noticeable in some countries than others. In France, Italy and Spain, where people continued to demand the best, eating of bread did not decline so sharply, although even in those countries, the quality did deteriorate for a time.

BELOW: In northern Europe, dark rye bread is served sliced with colourful, rich-tasting toppings.

BELOW: Cutting a cross in an unbaked loaf was believed to let the devil out.

In Britain, however, most bread was notoriously bland – the ubiquitous white sliced loaf being little more than a convenient shape for the toaster. In supermarkets, certainly, there was a time, not so long ago, when apart from the standard pre-wrapped white loaf, the only baked goods on sale were croissants and a selection of fruited teabreads, vaguely labelled as "Continental". Yet within the last twenty years, things have improved by leaps and bounds. Perhaps supermarkets, finding that the smell of freshly baked bread enticed shoppers into their stores, installed more in-store bakeries. Or perhaps shoppers who travelled abroad and sampled the breads of other countries created a demand for better breads made with better flours, using more imaginative recipes and untreated with additives.

Nowadays there is a huge choice of breads both from independent bakeries and from the large supermarkets. Italian ciabatta and focaccia are now a regular sight, even in the smallest food stores, as are the various Spanish, Indian and Middle Eastern breads. There is an increasingly interesting choice of German, Danish, Scandinavian and eastern European breads and, among the French breads, there is now a truly good range on offer. If the supermarket has an in-store bakery, baguettes are likely to be freshly baked and some are now as good as the real thing. The availability of *pain de campagnes*, *levains* and other rustic breads means that you can choose breads to suit the style of meal you are serving, while sweet breads, such as brioches and croissants from France, *pane al cioccolato* from Italy and numerous offerings from Germany mean that there is much more to choose from than simply toast at breakfast and malt loaf at tea time.

Local bakers, although competing with the supermarkets, have paradoxically benefited from the range on offer from supermarkets. The more breads there are available, the more people feel inclined to try other baked goods. Small bakers, who could easily have lost customers to the big stores, have risen to the challenge by producing their own range of country-style and fine breads. Craft bakers are

ABOVE: A huge range of traditionally baked French breads are offered for sale in this specialist bakery.

producing traditional breads, at the same time experimenting with recipes they have devised themselves. Bread making has never been a tradition that stood still. The best craft bakers have ensured that bread making has continued to evolve, resulting in the emergence of all sorts of corn and barley breads, mixed grain loaves and a range of new sourdoughs.

Added to this are the many European-style bakeries. Set up and run by émigrés from all parts of Europe and beyond, these bakeries are a great source of authentic European breads, as are local farmers markets. In supermarkets you will

BELOW: Traditional country-style breads are enjoying a renaissance.

invariably find ciabatta or focaccia, but for *paesano*, *pagnotta* or *pane sciocco* you are likely to need an Italian baker, who will be only too happy to provide you with the loaves and tell you all about them while they are being wrapped.

Once you have found a bakery you like, there are no particular tips for buying bread; the baker will be pleased to explain the different styles of loaves and advise on their keeping qualities. Crusty breads, such as baguettes, round cobs or Italian country loaves, are known as "oven bottom" or "oven bottom-baked", which means they have been baked, without tins (pans) or containers, on the sole of the oven or on flat sheet trays. They are evenly crusty, although the type of dough, the humidity during proving, the steam in the oven and the heat itself determines whether the crust is fragile or chewy. Loaves, such as the English farmhouse, baked in metal tins, characteristically have a golden top, but with thinner crusts on the sides. Rolls or breads baked up against each other have even softer sides and are described as "batch-baked". Sourdough breads are made without yeast – using a natural leaven instead – and are often labelled as "yeast-free" breads or "naturally leavened". There are many varieties, some made entirely from wheat, some from rye, others from a blend of both of these or other cereals. They are normally heavier than an average loaf, with a dense texture and pleasantly tart flavour.

INGREDIENTS FOR BREAD MAKING

WHEAT FLOURS

The simplest breads are a mixture of flour and water and some type of leavening agent. Beyond that narrow definition, however, lies an infinite number of possibilities. The flour is most likely to come from wheat, but may be derived from another type of grain or even, in the case of buckwheat, from another source entirely. The liquid may be water, but could just as easily be milk, or a mixture. Yeast is the obvious raising agent, but there are other options. Salt is normally essential, fats are often added, and other ingredients range from sweeteners like sugar or molasses to dried fruit, spices and savoury flavourings.

WHITE FLOUR

This flour contains about 75 per cent of the wheat grain with most of the bran and the wheat germ extracted. Plain flour is used for pastry, sauces and biscuits (cookies); while self-raising (self-rising) flour, which contains a raising agent, is used for cakes, scones (US biscuits) and puddings. It can also be used for soda bread. American all-purpose flour is a medium-strength flour, somewhere between the British plain and strong white flour. Soft flour, sometimes known as American cake flour, has been milled very finely for sponge cake and similar bakes.

UNBLEACHED WHITE FLOUR

Unbleached flour is more creamy in colour than other white flours, which have been whitened artificially. Bleaching, which involves treating the flour with chlorine, is becoming increasingly rare and the majority of white flours are unbleached, although check the packet to be sure. In Britain, flour producers are required by law to add, or fortify their white flours with, certain nutrients such as vitamin B1, nictinic acid, iron and calcium. These are often added in the form of white soya flour, which has a natural bleaching effect.

RIGHT: Organic flours are being used increasingly for bread making.

STRONG WHITE/WHITE BREAD FLOUR

For almost all bread making, the best type of flour to use is one which is largely derived from wheat that is high in protein. This type of flour is described as "strong" and is often labelled "bread flour", which underlines its suitability for the task. Proteins in the flour, when mixed with water, combine to make gluten and it is this that gives dough its elasticity when kneaded, and allows it to trap the bubbles of carbon dioxide given off by the yeast. A soft flour produces flat loaves that stale quickly; conversely, if the flour is too hard, the bread will have a coarse texture. A balance is required and most millers blend hard and soft wheats to make a flour that produces a well-flavoured loaf with good volume. Most strong white flours have a lower protein content than their wholemeal equivalent and a baker would probably use a flour with a protein level of 12 per cent. The protein value of a flour can be found listed on the side of the packet under "Nutritional Value".

FINE FRENCH PLAIN FLOUR

French bakers use a mixture of white bread flour and fine plain flour to make baguettes and other specialities. Fine French plain flour is called *farine fluide* in its country of origin because it is so light and free-flowing. Such is the popularity of French-style baked goods that this type of flour is now available in supermarkets.

WHOLEMEAL (WHOLE-WHEAT) FLOUR

This flour is made using the whole of the wheat grain and is sometimes called 100 per cent extraction flour: nothing is added and nothing is taken away. The bran and wheat germ, which are automatically separated from the white inner portion if milled between rollers, are returned to the white flour at the end of the process. *Atta* is a fine wholemeal flour used for Indian breads (see Other Flours).

STONEGROUND WHOLEMEAL FLOUR

This wholemeal flour has been ground in the traditional way between two stones. The bran and wheat germ are milled with the rest of the wheat grain, so there is no separation of the flour at any stage. Stoneground flour is also considered to have a better flavour, owing to the slow grinding of the stones. However, because the oily wheat germ is squashed into the flour, rather than churned in later, stoneground flour has a higher fat content and may become rancid if stored for too long.

ORGANIC WHOLEMEAL FLOUR

This flour has been milled from organic wheat, which is wheat produced without the use of artificial fertilizers or pesticides. There are organic versions of all varieties of wholemeal and white flours available from most large supermarkets and health-food stores.

STRONG WHOLEMEAL/ WHOLEMEAL BREAD FLOUR

A higher proportion of high gluten wheat is necessary in wholemeal flours to counteract the heaviness of the bran. If the flour is not strong enough, the dough may rise unevenly and is likely to collapse in the oven. The miller selects his grist (the blend) of hard and soft wheat grains, according to the type of flour required. Bakers would probably look for a protein content of about 13.5 per cent; the strong flours available in supermarkets are normally between 11.5 and 13 per cent.

ABOVE: Clockwise from top right: strong white flour, stoneground wholemeal, wholemeal, wheat germ, organic wholemeal, plain white flour, organic plain flour, semolina, organic stoneground wholemeal and Granary flour. The three flours in the centre are (clockwise from top) brown, spelt and self-raising flour.

GRANARY FLOUR

Granary (whole-wheat) is the proprietary name of a blend of brown and rye flours and malted wheat grain. The malted grain gives this bread its characteristic sweet and slightly sticky flavour and texture. It is available from health food stores and supermarkets.

MALTHOUSE FLOUR

A speciality flour available from some large supermarkets and health food stores, this is a combination of stoneground brown flour, rye flour and malted wheat flour with malted wheat flakes. It resembles Granary flour.

GRAHAM FLOUR

This popular American flour is slightly coarser than ordinary wholemeal. It is named after a 19th-century Connecticut cleric, Rev. Sylvestor Graham, who developed the flour and advocated using the whole grain for bread making because of the beneficial effects of the bran.

BROWN FLOUR

This flour contains about 85 per cent of the original grain, with some of the bran and wheat germ extracted. It produces a lighter loaf than 100 per cent wholemeal flour, while still retaining a high percentage of wheat germ, which gives bread so much of its flavour.

WHEAT GERM FLOUR

A wheat germ flour can be brown or white but must contain at least 10 per cent added wheat germ. Wheat germ is highly nutritious and this bread is considered particularly healthy. Wheat germ bread has a pleasant nutty flavour.

SEMOLINA

This is the wheat kernel once the bran and wheat germ have been removed from the grain by milling, but before it is fully milled into flour. Semolina can be ground either coarsely or finely and is used for certain Indian breads, including *bhatura*.

SPELT

Spelt flour contains more protein than wheat and is easier to digest, so some people who are allergic to wheat can tolerate spelt. It does contain gluten. It is available from some supermarkets and health food stores.

OTHER FLOURS

Alternative grains, such as barley, cornmeal and oatmeal, are full of flavour but contain little or no gluten. Breads made solely from them would rise poorly and would be extremely dense. The milled grains are therefore often mixed with strong wheat flour. Rye is rich in gluten, but pure rye doughs are difficult to handle; once again the addition of strong wheat flour can provide a solution.

BARLEY MEAL

Barley is low in gluten and is seldom used for bread making in Britain and western Europe. In Russia and other eastern European countries, however, barley loaves continue to be produced, the flour mostly blended with some proportion of wheat or rye flour to give the loaf volume. These loaves are definitely on the robust side. They tend to be rather grey and flat and have an earthy, rather mealy flavour. Similar loaves must have been baked in parts of the British Isles in the past, when times were hard or the wheat harvest had failed. There are several old Welsh recipes for barley bread, which was rolled out flat before being baked on a baking stone. Finnish barley bread is made in much the same way.

Barley meal is the ground whole grain of the barley, while barley flour is ground pearl barley, with the outer skin removed.

BELOW: Finnish barley bread

Either can be added in small quantities to wholemeal or to white flour to produce a bread with a slightly rustic flavour.

BUCKWHEAT FLOUR

This grain is blackish in colour, hence its French name, *blé noir*. It is not strictly a cereal but is the fruit of a plant belonging to the dock family. The three-cornered grains are milled to a flour and used for pancakes, blinis and, in France, for crêpes or galettes. It can also be added to wheat flour and is popular mixed with other grains in multigrained loaves. It has a distinctive, earthy flavour and is best used in small quantities.

CORN MEAL (MAIZEMEAL)

This meal is ground from white or yellow corn and is normally available in coarse, medium or fine grinds. Coarse-ground corn meal is used for the Italian dish of polenta; for bread making choose one of the finer grinds, available from most health food stores. There are numerous corn breads from the southern states of America, including the famous double corn bread. Corn was brought back to Europe by the Spanish and Portuguese and corn breads are still popular in these countries today, particularly in Portugal. Corn contains no gluten so will not make a loaf unless it is blended with wheat flour, in which case the corn adds a pleasant flavour and colour.

MILLET FLOUR

Although high in protein, millet flour is low in gluten and is not commonly used by itself in bread making. It is pale yellow in colour, with a gritty texture. The addition of wheat flour produces an interesting, slightly nutty flavour.

OATMEAL

Oatmeal does not contain gluten and is only very rarely used by itself for bread making. The exception is in Scotland where flat crisply baked oatmeal biscuits have been popular for centuries. These are baked on a griddle and served with butter or marmalade. Oatmeal can also be used in wheat or multigrained loaves. Choose finely ground oatmeal for making oatcakes or for using in loaves. Rolled oats are not a flour but are the steamed and flattened whole oats. They look good scattered over the crust of leaves and rolls, and add a pleasant flavour.

RICE FLOUR

Polished rice, if ground very finely, becomes rice flour. It can be used as a thickening agent and is useful for people with wheat allergies. It is also occasionally used for some Indian breads.

STORAGE

Although most flours keep well, they do not last indefinitely and it is important to pay attention to the "use-by" date on the packet. Old flour will begin to taste stale and will make a disappointing loaf. Always store flour on a cool dry shelf. Ideally, the flour should be kept in its bag and placed in a tin or storage jar with a tight-fitting lid. Wash and dry the jar thoroughly whenever replacing with new flour and avoid adding new flour to old. Wholemeal (whole-wheat) flour, because it contains the oils in wheatgerm, keeps less well than white flours. Consequently, do not buy large quantities at a time and keep it in a very cool place or in the salad drawer of the refrigerator.

ABOVE: A selection of non-wheat grains and specialist flours. Clockwise from top centre: rye flour, buckwheat flour, corn meal, bajra flour, organic rye flour, millet grain, jowar flour, gram flour and atta or chapati flour. In the centre are (clockwise from top) barley meal, fine oatmeal and rice flour.

RYE FLOUR

Rye is the only other cereal, apart from wheat, that is widely used to make bread. It has a good gluten content, although the gluten in rye is different from wheat gluten, and rye doughs are notoriously sticky and difficult to handle. For this reason, rye meal is often blended with other flours to create a dough that is more manageable. There are as many different rye meals as there are wheat flours, ranging in colour and in type of grind. Pumpernickel and other dense and steamed box-shaped rye breads use a coarsely ground wholemeal rye, while finer flour, which contains neither the bran nor the germ, is used for the popular crusty black breads.

INDIAN FLOURS
ATTA/CHAPATI FLOUR

This is a very fine wholemeal (whole-wheat) flour, which is normally found only in Indian grocers where it is sometimes labelled *ata*. As well as being used to make chapatis, it is also the type of flour used for making rotis and other Indian flat breads.

BAJRA FLOUR

This plant grows along the west coast of India. The grains are a mixture of yellow and grey but when ground, the flour is a more uniform grey. It has a strong nutty aroma and a distinct flavour. *Bajra* bread or *rotla* is cooked, like all unleavened breads, on a griddle.

JOWAR FLOUR

Jowar grows over most of central and southern India. The flour, ground from the pretty pale yellow grains, is a creamy-white colour. The flat breads usually made from this flour, called *bhakris*, are roasted on a griddle and are traditionally served with a rich-flavoured, spicy, coconut, garlic and red chilli chutney.

GRAM FLOUR

This is a flour made from ground chickpeas. It is also known as *besan*. The Indian missi rotis – spicy, unleavened breads from northern India – are made using gram flour or a mixture of wholewheat and gram flours.

YEAST AND OTHER LEAVENS

Almost all breads today are leavened in some way, which means that a substance has been added to the dough to initiate fermentation and make the dough rise.

Without yeast or another leavening agent, the mixture of flour and water, once cooked, would be merely a flat, unappetizing cake. At some point in our history, our ancestors discovered how dough, if left to ferment in the warmth, produced a lighter and airier bread when cooked.

The transformation of dough into bread is caused by yeast or another leavening ingredient producing carbon dioxide. The carbon dioxide expands, the dough stretches and tiny pockets of air are introduced into the dough. When the bread is cooked the process is set and the air becomes locked in.

LEAVENING AGENTS
The most popular and most widely known leavening ingredient in bread making is yeast. However, raising agents such as

BELOW: Clockwise from top left: fresh yeast, dried yeast, fast-action bread yeast and easy bake dried yeast.

bicarbonate of soda (baking soda) and baking powder are also used for making certain breads.

YEAST
Yeast is the most popular leavening agent for bread making. It is simple to use, more reliable than a natural leaven and considerably quicker to activate. Conventional dried yeast, easy bake (rapid-rise) and fast-action bread yeast are all types of dried yeast, produced for the convenience of those making bread at home. Almost all bakers prefer fresh yeast, since it is considered to have a superior flavour and to be more reliable. However, when fresh yeast is not available or convenient, dried yeast is a handy substitute.

There are several ways of adding yeast to flour. Fresh yeast is usually blended with lukewarm water before being mixed into the flour; conventional dried yeast is first reconstituted in warm water and then left until frothy; easy bake and fast-action bread yeasts are added directly to the flour.

THE SPONGE METHOD
Some yeasted breads are made by the sponge method, whereby the yeast is dissolved in more lukewarm water than usual, and then mixed with

some of the flour to make a batter. This can be done in a bowl, or the batter can be made in a well in the centre of the flour, with only some surrounding flour included at the start, as in the recipe for split tin loaf. The batter is left for at least 20 minutes – often much longer – until bubbles appear on the surface, a process known as sponging. It is then mixed with the remaining flour, and any other ingredients are added. The advantage of this method is that it enables the yeast to start working without being inhibited by ingredients like eggs, fat and sugar, which slow down its action.

Many French breads are also sponged. A slightly different technique is used and the batter is left to ferment for a lot longer – for 2–12 hours. The slow fermentation creates what is described as a *poolish* sponge, and makes for a wonderfully flavoured bread, with very little acidity, yet with a fragile and crunchy crust. *Pain polka* is made by this method, as are the best baguettes. Two factors affect the rise: the temperature of the room and the wetness of the mixture. A wet sponge will rise more quickly than a firmer one. Italian bakers employ a similar process called a *biga*. This uses less liquid and the sponge takes about 12–15 hours to mature. For an example of the use of a *biga* starter, see the recipe for ciabatta.

BAKING POWDER
This is made up of a mixture of acid and alkaline chemicals. When these come into contact with moisture, as in a dough or a batter, the reaction of the chemicals produces tiny bubbles of air so the dough rises and becomes spongy, just as it does with yeast. Unlike when making yeast-leavened breads, however, it is important to work fast as the carbon dioxide will quickly escape and the loaf will collapse.

BICARBONATE OF SODA
Bicarbonate of soda (baking soda), sometimes just called soda, is the leavening ingredient in Irish soda bread. It is an alkaline chemical which, when mixed with an

acid in a moisture-rich environment, reacts to produce carbon dioxide. Cream of tartar, an acid that is made from fermented grapes, is commonly used in conjunction with bicarbonate of soda for soda breads, or else the soda is combined with soured milk, which is naturally acidic. Buttermilk may also be used.

BREWER'S YEAST

Old cookbooks sometimes call for brewer's yeast or ale or beer barm. Until the last century, this was the common and only leavening ingredient. Since then brewer's yeast has acquired something of a cult status, and during the 1950s in the USA and Britain it was considered a wonder food owing to its nutritional value. It is not however, suitable for bread making, being too bitter, and should only be used for making beer.

NATURAL LEAVENS

Natural leavens, made using a medium of flour, or grown from potatoes, yogurt, treacle or buttermilk, were once very popular and are enjoying a renaissance.

SOURDOUGHS

Sourdoughs are breads based on a natural leaven. An authentic sourdough relies entirely on the wild yeasts that exist in the air. Given the right conditions, any dough of flour and water or batter of vegetable origin will start to ferment spontaneously and will continue to do so if starch or sugar is added to feed it. Recipes for some of the traditional American and German breads use a variety of rather surprising starters for their sourdoughs, from potatoes to treacle. With the renewed interest in rustic breads, there are all sorts of sourdough breads in supermarkets and specialist bakers, and numerous books explaining how to make them at home.

There are many, many types of sourdough. In France the sourdough method is known as the *chef* or *levain*, and is used

LEFT: *Pain de campagne is one of the many French sourdough breads.*

for *pain de campagne* as well as for sourdough baguettes.

Despite their many variations, sourdoughs do have some elements in common. Each begins with a "starter", which can take anything up to a week to ferment and become established. This "starter" or leaven is used, daily by bakers or less frequently by home bread makers, for the day's bread. A small amount of the dough is then kept back and used for the next batch of bread. Alternatively, a slightly more liquid starter

can be made and kept in the refrigerator until it is ready for use. Each time part of the starter is used, the remaining starter is refreshed with equal amounts of flour and water. Looked after in this way, some starters have been known to survive for many years. Starters for sourdoughs, as well as the breads themselves, vary hugely – not only from country to country but from village to village. Many recipes, and indeed many bakers, recommend using a little yeast to get started since a true starter is likely to be rather a hit-or-miss affair. Wild yeasts may be all around us, but for some reason they seem to vanish as soon as you decide to make a sourdough. Starters also improve with age, so do not be discouraged if your first sourdoughs are rather bland. After a few attempts, you should find your breads developing their own tangy personality.

YEAST KNOW-HOW

◆ Yeast needs warmth to activate it, but must not be subjected to too hot a temperature or it will die. Whether dissolving yeast in water or adding liquid to the yeast and flour, make sure the liquid is not too warm. The optimum heat is 38°C/100°F. If you do not have a thermometer, experts recommend mixing 300ml/½ pint/1¼ cups boiling water with 600ml/1pint/2½ cups cold water, and measuring the required water from the mixture.

◆ If you are using easy bake or fast-action dried bread yeast you can afford to have the water slightly hotter, since the yeast is mixed with the flour, and the heat of the water will rapidly dissipate.

◆ Check "use-by" dates on dried and fast-action yeasts. If a product is past its "use-by" date, replace it. If it is marginal and you cannot immediately replace it, take a measuring jug (cup)

and pour in 120ml/4fl oz/½ cup warm water (43–46°C/110–115°F). Add 5ml/1 tsp sugar, stir to dissolve and then sprinkle over 10ml/2 tsp dried yeast. Stir and leave for 10 minutes. The yeast should begin to rise to the surface after the first 5 minutes, and by 10 minutes there should have developed a rounded crown of foam that reaches to the 250ml/8fl oz/1 cup level of the measuring jug. If this happens the yeast is active; if not, the yeast has lost its potency and should be discarded.

◆ The amount of yeast you require should not increase proportionally as the amount of flour increases, so take care if you decide to double the quantities in a recipe. You will not need to double the amount of yeast. Similarly, if you halve a recipe, you are likely to need proportionally more yeast or be prepared to wait longer for the bread to rise.

ADDITIONAL INGREDIENTS

ABOVE: Welsh bara brith is packed with dried fruits.

SUGAR

Sugar, once invariably added to all breads (usually with the yeast), is now no longer necessary for savoury breads since modern yeasts can be activated without it. However, some bakers still prefer to add a little sugar, even when making savoury baked goods, contending that results with sugar are better than when it is omitted.

White and brown sugar, honey, treacle (molasses) and golden (light corn) syrup can be used to sweeten teabreads and fruit breads. Sugars are normally added with the flour, while syrups are more often stirred into the lukewarm liquid so that they are gently warmed as well.

BUTTER AND EGGS

Enriched breads are made with the addition of both butter and eggs and normally use milk rather than water. These breads, such as Sally Lunn, barm brack and many of the festive European breads, have a delicious cake-like texture and soft crust. The butter is either melted or diced and the eggs beaten before being worked into other ingredients to make a fairly sticky batter. This is then beaten by hand or in an electric mixer. In some instances, the butter is kneaded into the dough after the initial rising, since large quantities of butter can inhibit the action of the yeast.

Although flour and yeast are the most obvious ingredients used in bread making, there are a number of other ingredients that are just as important.

WATER OR MILK

As a general rule, savoury loaves are made using water; teabreads and sweeter breads use milk. Whatever the liquid, it is always heated slightly. Breads made with milk are softer in both the crumb and the crust than those using water.

SALT

Almost all bread recipes add salt at the beginning, stirring or sifting it right into the flour.

Salt is one of the few essential ingredients in bread making. It is important for both flavour and the effect it has on the yeast and dough. Essentially, it slows down the yeast's action – which is why it should not be added directly to the yeast. This means that the dough rises in a controlled and even way, giving a well-risen even loaf. Too little salt means the loaf will stale more quickly; too much and the crust will harden, so do take care when measuring salt.

LEFT: The French petit pains au lait, made with milk rather than water, have a lovely soft crumb and crust.

BELOW: Sally Lunn, one of the richest breads of all, is traditionally served sandwiched with clotted cream.

ABOVE: Panettone is enriched with eggs and egg yolks.

BELOW: Red lentil dosas are spiced with turmeric and black pepper.

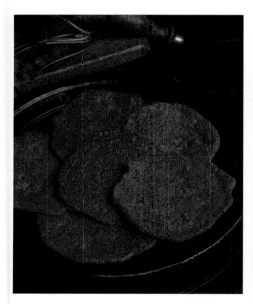

FRUIT

Almost any dried fruit can be added to bread. Raisins, sultanas (golden raisins), currants and mixed (candied) peel have always been popular for fruit loaves. Chopped dates, apricots and prunes can all be kneaded in, as can more exotic fruits, such as dried mango or papaya. Fruit can be added to a dough during mixing or left until the second kneading. If adding at the second kneading, warm the fruit first, so that it does not inhibit the action of the yeast. If you are using an electric mixer or food processor for kneading, note that the blades will chop the fruit. This spoils both the appearance and the flavour of the loaf, so only knead by machine to begin with, then knead the fruit in by hand after the initial rising.

FATS

Fats, in the form of butter, oil, lard (shortening) or vegetable fat, are sometimes added to savoury loaves. They add flavour and help to preserve the freshness of the loaf. The Italians particularly love adding olive oil to their breads, which they do in generous quantities. Although oils and melted butter can be poured into the flour with the yeast and liquid, solid butter or fats are normally kneaded into the flour before the liquid is added.

NUTS, HERBS AND OTHER SAVOURY INGREDIENTS

Some of our favourite breads today are flavoured with herbs, nuts and other

BELOW: Ciabatta, like many Italian breads, is made with olive oil.

such savoury ingredients. *Manoucher*, "Mediterranean nights" bread, is a rainbow of colours. Based on the Italian *focaccia*, it contains rosemary, red, green and yellow (bell) peppers along with goat's cheese. The Italians add olives or sun-dried tomatoes to their ciabatta, while walnut bread (*pain aux noix* in France, *pane con noci* in Italy) is one of the best-known and best-loved savoury loaves.

Nuts, herbs, pitted olives and sun-dried tomatoes should be roughly chopped before being kneaded into the dough after the first rising.

SPICES

The sweet spices are cinnamon, nutmeg, cloves and ginger, and for savoury breads cumin, fennel, caraway and anise impart a delicious flavour. Mace, pepper and coriander seeds can be used for both sweet and savoury breads. Spices can be added with the flour or kneaded in with fruit or nuts, or other ingredients.

TECHNIQUES

USING YEAST

There are several different forms of yeast, some easier to use than others, but none of them particularly tricky if you follow a few simple rules. Whichever yeast you use, it must be in good condition – neither old nor stale – and must not be subjected to too much heat.

USING FRESH YEAST

Fresh yeast is available from baker's stores, health food stores and most supermarkets with an in-store bakery. It is pale beige, has a sweet, fruity smell and should crumble easily. It can be stored in the refrigerator, wrapped in clear film (plastic wrap), for up to 2 weeks or can be frozen for up to 3 months. A quantity of 15g/½oz fresh yeast should be sufficient for 675–900g/ 1½–2lb/6–8 cups flour, although this will depend on the recipe.

1 Put the yeast in a small bowl. Using a spoon, mash or "cream" it with a little of the measured water until smooth.

2 Pour in the remaining measured liquid, which may be water, milk or a mixture of the two. Mix well. Use as directed in the recipe.

USING DRIED YEAST

Dried yeast is simply the dehydrated equivalent of fresh yeast, but it needs to be blended with lukewarm liquid before use. Store dried yeast in a cool dry place and check the "use-by" date on the can or packet. You will need about 15g/½oz (7.5ml/1½ tsp) dried yeast for 675g/ 1½lb/6 cups flour. Some bakers add sugar or honey to the liquid to which the yeast is added, but this is not necessary, as the granules contain enough nourishment to enable the yeast to work.

1 Pour the measured lukewarm liquid into a small bowl and sprinkle the dried yeast evenly over the surface.

2 Cover with clear film and leave in a warm room for 10–15 minutes until frothy. Stir well and use as directed.

WATER TEMPERATURE

For fresh and regular dried yeast, use lukewarm water; for easy-blend and fast-action yeast the water can be a little hotter, as the yeast is mixed with flour before the liquid is added.

USING EASY BAKE (RAPID-RISE) AND FAST-ACTION DRIED BREAD YEASTS

These are the most convenient of the dried yeasts as they can be stirred directly into the flour. Fast-action bread yeasts and easy bake dried yeasts usually contain a bread improver, which eliminates the need for two kneadings and risings – check the instructions on the packet to make sure. Most of these yeasts come in 7g/¼oz sachets, which are sufficient for 675g/1½lb/6 cups flour. Do not store opened sachets as the yeast will deteriorate quickly.

Sift together the flour and salt into a medium bowl and rub in the fat, if using. Stir in the easy bake or fast-action dried bread yeast, then add warm water or milk, plus any other ingredients, as directed in the recipe.

BELOW: Small, shaped rolls are very quick to make using easy-blend yeast.

Making a Yeast Dough by the Sponge Method

This method produces bread with an excellent flavour and soft texture. The quantities listed are merely an example and can be increased proportionately. See individual recipes.

1 Mix 7g/¼oz fresh yeast with 250ml/8fl oz/1 cup lukewarm water in a large bowl. Stir in 115g/4oz/1 cup unbleached plain (all-purpose) flour, using a wooden spoon, then use your fingers to draw the mixture together until you have a smooth liquid with the consistency of a thick batter. (Do not add salt to the sponge as this would inhibit the yeast.)

2 Cover with a damp dishtowel and leave in a warm place. The sponge will double or triple in bulk and then fall back, which indicates it is ready to use (after about 5–6 hours).

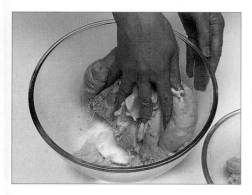

3 The sponge starter is now ready to be mixed to a dough with the remaining flour and any other ingredients, such as butter as directed in the recipe.

MAKING AN ITALIAN STARTER (*BIGA*)

If you wish to make an Italian *biga* for Pugliese or a similar Italian country bread, use 175g/6oz/1½ cups unbleached plain flour. Cream the yeast with 90ml/6 tbsp lukewarm water, then pour it into a well in the centre of the flour. Gradually mix in the surrounding flour to form a firm dough. The dough should be kneaded for a few minutes and then left, covered with lightly oiled clear film (plastic wrap) for 12–15 hours.

Making a French Sourdough Starter (*Chef*)

It is not difficult to make a sourdough starter. The starter can be kept in the refrigerator for up to 10 days, but for longer than that it should be frozen. Bring the starter to room temperature before adding to the next batch of bread.

1 Place 115g/4oz/1 cup flour in a large bowl and add 75ml/5 tbsp water. Mix together, then knead for 3–4 minutes to form a dough. Cover the bowl with clear film and set aside at room temperature for 2–3 days. The flour that you choose will depend on the bread you wish to make; it can be wholemeal (whole-wheat), white or rye, or a combination of two or three.

2 After 2–3 days, the mixture will rise and aerate slightly and turn a greyish colour. A soft crust may form on top of the starter and it should develop a slightly sweet-sour smell.

3 Remove any crust that has formed on top of the starter and discard. Stir in 120ml/4fl oz/½ cup lukewarm water to make a paste and then add 175g/6oz/1½ cups flour. The flour can be wholemeal or a mixture of wholemeal and white. Mix together to make a dough, then transfer to a work surface and knead lightly until firm.

SOURDOUGH

The actual word "sourdough" is thought to have come from America as this style of bread was commonly made by pioneers and the word was sometimes used to describe old "Forty-Niners". However bread made by the sourdough method dates back long before the 19th century. Many traditional European rye breads are based on this method, particularly in Germany and Scandinavia where the sour flavour of the leaven complements the flavour of the rye.

In Britain sourdoughs are sometimes called acids or acid breads. Some restaurants and home bread makers have their own favourite acid breads, but generally there is not much of a tradition of sourdoughs in the British Isles. Except in Ireland, where soda was popular, ale barm (the fermentation liquor from beer) was the most commonly used leaven for bread making until it was replaced by baker's yeast around the middle of the last century.

4 Place the ball of dough in a bowl, cover again with clear film and leave for 1–2 days at room temperature.

5 Remove and discard any crust that forms. What remains – the *chef* – can now be used to make a sourdough bread, such as *pain de campagne rustique*. To keep the *chef* going, save about 225g/8oz of the dough each time.

6 Place the dough starter in a crock or bowl, cover and keep in the refrigerator for up to 10 days or freeze.

MIXING, KNEADING AND RISING

The sequence and method of adding ingredients to make your dough are vital. For some breads, fresh or dried yeast is dissolved in lukewarm water and then stirred into the flour; if easy bake (rapid-rise) dried yeast or fast-action dried bread yeast is used, then add the warm water or milk added afterwards. Read your recipe carefully before starting and warm your bowls if they are in the least bit chilly, so that the yeast gets off to a good start.

MIXING

The easiest way to mix the dough is with your hand but, if you prefer, start mixing with a spoon until the mixture is too stiff to stir, then mix by hand.

1 If using fresh or regular dried yeast, mix it with lukewarm water or milk as described in the recipe. Sift the flour, salt and any other dry ingredients (including easy bake or fast-action dried yeast, if using) into a large, warm mixing bowl.

2 If using butter or lard (shortening), rub it in. Make a well in the centre of the flour mixture and pour in the yeast mixture with the remaining lukewarm water. If oil is being used, add it now.

3 Mix the liquid into the flour using your hand, stirring in a smooth, wide motion so that all the dry ingredients are evenly incorporated and the mixture forms a dough. Knead lightly in the bowl.

KNEADING

Kneading is something you just cannot skip in bread making. If you do not have strong wrists, or simply do not enjoy it, you will have to resort to using the food processor, which takes all the effort – and much of the time – out of kneading. Better still though, learn to love it.

Kneading dough, whether by hand or machine, is the only way of warming and stretching the gluten in the flour. As the strands of gluten warm and become more elastic, so the dough becomes more springy. It is the elasticity of the dough, combined with the action of the yeast, that gives bread its light, springy texture. Insufficient kneading means that the dough cannot hold the little pockets of air, and the bread will collapse in the oven to leave a heavy and dense loaf.

HOW TO KNEAD BY HAND

1 Place the mixed dough on a floured surface and flour your hands generously.

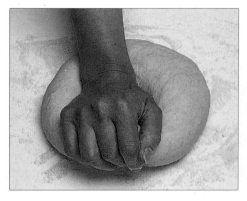

2 Press the heel of your hand firmly into the centre of the dough, then curl your fingers around the edge of the dough.

3 Pull and stretch the dough towards you and press down again, giving the dough a quarter turn as you do so.

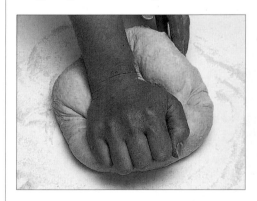

4 Continue pressing and stretching the dough, making quarter turns so that it is evenly kneaded. After about 10 minutes the dough should be supple and elastic; however, some breads need more kneading, so do check the recipe.

ADDING EXTRA INGREDIENTS

Ingredients, such as olives, can be added after kneading, or they can be kneaded in after the first rising.

KNEADING IN A FOOD PROCESSOR

Unless you have an industrial-size machine, it is likely that your food processor will only be able to knead moderate amounts of dough. Don't attempt to knead more dough than recommended by the manufacturer as it may damage the motor. If necessary, knead in small batches and then knead the dough balls together by hand afterwards.

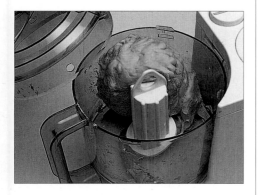

Fit the dough blade into the processor and then blend together all the dry ingredients. Add the yeast mixture, and extra lukewarm liquid and butter or oil, if required; process until the mixture comes together. Knead for 60 seconds, or according to the manufacturer's instructions, then knead by hand on a floured board for 1–2 minutes.

KNEADING IN A FOOD MIXER

Check the manufacturer's instructions to make sure bread dough can be kneaded in your machine.

Mix the dry ingredients together. Add the yeast, liquid and oil or butter, if using, and mix slowly, using the dough hook. The dough will tumble and fall to begin with, and then it will slowly come together. Continue kneading the dough for 3–4 minutes or according to the manufacturer's instructions.

RISING

This is the easy part of bread making – all you need now is to give the dough the right conditions, and nature and chemistry will do the rest. While kneading works and conditions the gluten in the flour, during rising the yeast does the work. The fermentation process creates carbon dioxide, which is trapped within the dough by the elastic gluten. This process also has the effect of conditioning the flour, improving the flavour and texture of the eventual loaf.

The number of times you leave your bread to rise will depend on the yeast you are using and the recipe. An easy bake or a fast-action dried bread yeast needs no first rising, but dough using fresh yeast and other dried yeasts normally requires two risings, with some recipes calling for even more.

TEMPERATURE AND TIME

For most recipes, dough is left to rise at a temperature of about 24–27°C/75–80°F, the equivalent of an airing cupboard or near a warm oven. At a cooler temperature the bread rises more slowly and some of the best-flavoured breads, including baguettes, use a slower rising, giving the enzymes and starches in the flour more time to mature. The quantity of yeast used will also determine the time required for rising. More yeast means quicker rising.

1 Place the kneaded dough in a bowl that has been lightly greased. This will prevent the dough from sticking. Cover the bowl with a damp dishtowel or a piece of oiled clear film (plastic wrap), to prevent a skin from forming on top.

2 Leave to rise until the dough has doubled in bulk. At room temperature, this should take 1½–2 hours – less if the temperature is warmer; more if the room is cool. It can even be left to rise in the refrigerator for about 8 hours.

A FEW SIMPLE RULES

◆ Warm bowls and other equipment.

◆ Use the correct amount of yeast: too much will speed up the rising process but will spoil the flavour and will mean the loaf stales more quickly.

◆ If you have a thermometer, check the temperature of the lukewarm liquid, at least until you can gauge it accurately yourself. It should be between 37–43°C/98–108°F. Mixing two parts cold water with one part boiling water gives you water at roughly the right temperature.

◆ The amount of liquid required for a dough depends on several factors – type of flour, other ingredients, even the room temperature. Recipes therefore often give approximate quantities of liquid. You will soon learn to judge the ideal consistency of a dough.

◆ Do not skimp on kneading. Kneading is essential for stretching the gluten to give a well-risen, light-textured loaf.

◆ Avoid leaving dough to rise in a draught and make sure the ambient temperature is not too high, or the dough will begin to cook.

◆ Always cover the bowl during rising as a crust will form on top of the dough if the air gets to it. Clear film can be pressed on to the dough itself or can be stretched over the bowl. Either way, oil the film first or the dough will stick to it as it rises.

◆ Remember: the slower the rising, the better the taste of the bread.

KNOCKING BACK, SHAPING AND FINAL RISING

KNOCKING BACK

After all the effort by the yeast to create a risen dough, it seems a shame to knock it back. However, this process not only redistributes the gases in the dough that were created by fermentation, it also rein-vigorates the yeast, making sure that it is evenly distributed, and ensures the bread has an even texture. It should take only a few minutes and the bread is then ready for shaping. The dough is fully risen when it has doubled in bulk. If you are not sure that it is ready, test by gently inserting a finger into the centre of the dough. The dough should not immediately spring back. If it does, leave for a little longer.

1 Knock back the risen dough using your knuckles. Americans call this "punching down the dough", which is an accurate description of the process. Having knocked back the dough, place it on a floured work surface and knead lightly for 1–2 minutes.

SHAPING

There are several ways of shaping the dough to fit a loaf tin (pan).

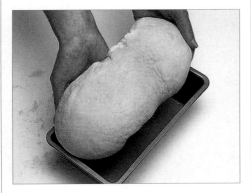

1 The easiest way is to shape the dough roughly into an oval and place it in the tin, with the smooth side on top.

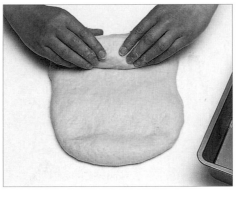

2 Alternatively, roll out the dough into a rectangle, a little longer than the tin. Roll it up like a Swiss roll, tuck in the ends and place the roll in the tin, with the seam side down.

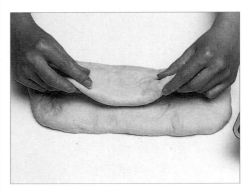

3 Another method for shaping the dough is to roll it out into a rectangle and fold it in half lengthways, pinching the edges together on the sides and flattening the dough out slightly with the heel of your hand. Fold the dough over once more to make a double thickness and pinch the edges together again. Now gently roll the dough backwards and forwards until it has a well-rounded shape.

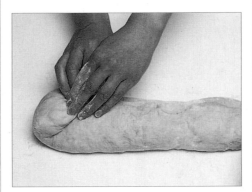

4 Fold in the two short ends and place the dough in the prepared tin with the seam along the bottom.

1 Shape the dough into a round and then press along the centre with your hand. Turn the dough over, so that the smooth side is uppermost.

2 Shape the dough into a round or oval and place it on a baking sheet.

TIPS

◆ Always knock back the dough after the first rising and knead lightly to redistribute the yeast and the gases formed by fermentation, otherwise you may end up with large holes in the loaf or the crust may lift up and become detached from the crumb.

◆ Rising the dough in a warm place is not always necessary – it is simply a method of speeding up the process. Dough will rise (albeit very slowly) even in the refrigerator. However, wherever you decide to rise your dough the temperature must be constant. Avoid draughts or hot spots, as both will spoil the bread and may cause it to bake unevenly.

◆ Some breads may need slashing either before final rising or during this period (see next section).

SHAPING A BAGUETTE

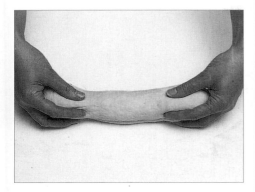

1 Divide the dough into equal pieces. Shape each piece into a ball and then into a rectangle measuring 15 × 7.5cm/ 6 × 3in. Fold the bottom third up and the top third down lengthways. Press the edges together to seal them. Repeat twice, then stretch each piece to a 33–35cm/13–14in loaf.

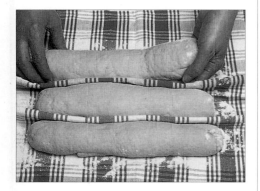

2 Place within the folds of a pleated, floured dishtowel or in *bannetons*.

SHAPING A PLAIT

1 Divide the dough into three equal pieces. Roll each piece into a 25cm/10in sausage about 4cm/1½in thick.

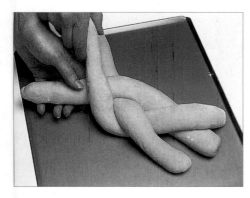

2 Place the three "sausages" on a greased baking sheet. Either start the plait (braid) in the centre, plaiting to each end in turn, or pinch the pieces firmly together at one end then plait.

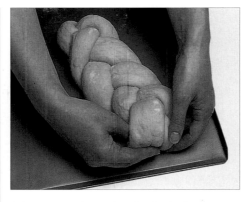

3 When you have finished, pinch the ends together, and turn them under.

FINAL RISING

After shaping the dough and placing it on the baking sheet or in the tin (pan), there is usually a final rising before baking. Depending on the warmth of the room, this can take ¾–1½ hours and in a very cool room up to 4 hours. Cover the dough so that the surface does not crust over. Oiled clear film (plastic wrap) placed over the tin or directly on the bread is best. The timing is important as over-rising means the loaf may collapse in the oven, while too little proving will mean the loaf will be heavy and flat.

BELOW: A loaf ready for the final rising.

BELOW: After rising the dough should be double in size – no more.

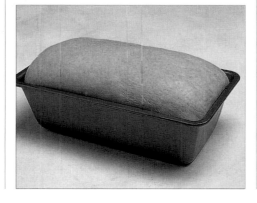

COOK'S TIP
When stretching dough for baguettes or plaits, work with care so that you don't overstretch it. If the dough feels as if it is going to tear, leave that strand to rest for a minute or two and work on one of the other pieces of dough. When you go back to the first piece, you will find that the gluten has allowed the dough to stretch and you can work it some more.

PROVING BASKETS

Professional bakers use proving baskets called *bannetons* for baguettes, and circular *couronnes* for round loaves. Some are lined with linen. Proving baskets are available from good kitchenware shops but, depending on the shape you require, you can improvise with baskets and/or earthenware dishes. Simply dust a linen dishtowel liberally with flour and use to line the container.

BELOW: A proving basket will give your loaves a professional finish.

CHOOSING TINS

Choosing the right size of loaf tin (pan) can be tricky. If it is too small the dough will spill over the top. If it is too large, the final loaf will be uneven. As a rule the tin should be about twice the size of the dough. Professional bakers use black tins, which are considered to be better than shiny metal ones as they absorb the heat better, giving a crisper crust. Always warm a tin before using and then grease it with melted lard (shortening), vegetable oil or unsalted (sweet) butter. Experiment to see what you find most successful. Baking sheets should also be greased to prevent sticking.

TOPPING AND BAKING

The actual baking is perhaps the simplest part of the bread-making process, yet even here the yeast still has a part to play and it is important that you play your part too, by making sure conditions are as ideal as possible. When the loaf goes into the oven the heat kills the yeast, but for the first few minutes, there is a final burst of life and the bread will rise even further before the entire process is set and the air is finally locked in.

PREPARING TO BAKE

While the shaped dough is having its final rise, you will need to preheat the oven to the required temperature. It is important that the oven is at the right temperature when the bread goes in – almost always a hot oven, between 220–230°C/425–450°F/ Gas 7–8, although check the recipe since sweet loaves or those containing a lot of butter cook at a lower temperature. Many recipes suggest that the oven temperature is reduced either immediately after putting the bread in the oven or some time during cooking. This means the bread gets a good blast of heat to start with, and then cooks more gradually. This mimics the original bread ovens, which would have cooled down slowly once the embers had been removed.

SLASHING

Once the loaf is ready for baking, all that is needed is to slash and glaze the loaf. This is done not only for appearance, but also to improve the baking of the loaf. When the loaf goes into the oven, the yeast will continue to produce carbon dioxide for a short time and the loaf will rise. This is called the "spring". Slashing provides escape routes for the gas and gives direction to the spring, so that the loaf will open out around the slashes and retain an even shape. Loaves that have not been allowed enough time to rise will tend to have more spring, and it is therefore important to slash these fairly deeply. If you think your loaf may have over-risen, only slash it gently.

You will also find that some recipes suggest slashing either before the final rising

or some time during it. This will depend on how much you want your loaf to "open up". The earlier it is slashed the more the split will develop. However, unless the recipe specifies otherwise, the general rule is to slash the loaf just before you put it in the oven.

ABOVE: Cob or coburg – just before baking, slash a deep cross across the top of the loaf.

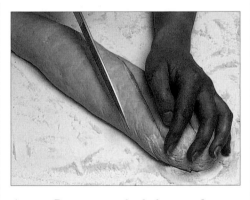

ABOVE: Baguette – slash four or five times on the diagonal just before the baking process.

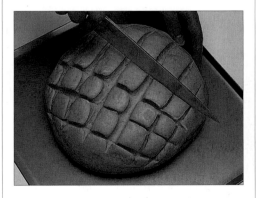

ABOVE: Porcupine – slashing not only looks attractive, but gives a wonderful crunchy crust to this bread. Make five or six cuts across the bread in one direction, then cut again at right angles, chequerboard fashion.

ABOVE: Tin loaf – part-way through rising, make one deep slash along the length of the loaf.

GLAZING

Glazing has two important functions. It gives an attractive finish to the loaf and it introduces moisture during cooking. This moisture produces steam which also helps to expand the gases in the loaf and ensures it cooks through completely. Glazes also change the consistency and taste of the crust. Bread can be glazed before, during or just after baking: sometimes recipes will suggest all three. If you glaze before and during baking, take care not to brush sticky glazes up to the sides of a tin (pan) or let the glaze drip on to the baking sheet, thereby gluing the bread to its container. This will cause the loaf to crack and rise unevenly.

All sorts of glazes can be used – egg yolk, egg white, milk, butter, sugar solutions, salt solutions and olive oil are regularly used. They also help the toppings to stick to the surface of the loaf.

ABOVE: Brushing a plait (braid) with beaten egg yolk and milk before baking gives it a golden glaze and a professional-looking finish.

TOPPINGS

There are as many toppings as there are glazes, if not more, all of which add to the appearance, taste and texture of your finished bread. The dough can be rolled in a topping before the second rising, or it can be glazed and sprinkled with the topping just before baking. Try poppy seeds, grated cheese, caraway seeds, oats, cracked wheat, sea salt, sunflower seeds, sesame seeds, herbs, cornmeal or wheat flakes as alternative toppings.

For basic breads and rolls, toppings are simply a matter of preference – for dinner parties offer people a selection of white and wholemeal (whole-wheat) rolls, each sprinkled with a different topping. Some breads classically have their own particular topping. *Challah*, for instance, is traditionally sprinkled with poppy seeds, pretzels are covered with sea salt or caraway seeds, while the long thin grissini can be rolled in either sesame or poppy seeds. Rolled oats add a soft texture to loaves, and many traditional British and American loaves, such as English cottage

ABOVE: Roll the dough for a Granary loaf in sunflower seeds.

ABOVE: A split tin loaf can be dusted with flour before baking.

ABOVE: Grated cheese

ABOVE: Cornmeal

ABOVE: Cracked wheat

ABOVE: Chopped fresh herbs

ABOVE: Rolled oats

ABOVE: Chopped black olives

ABOVE: Poppy seeds

ABOVE: Sea salt

ABOVE: Sesame seeds

ABOVE: Wheat flakes

ABOVE: Sunflower seeds

ABOVE: Caraway seeds

loaf and San Francisco sourdough bread, have no toppings as such, but a dusting of flour gives an attractive matt sheen to the finished loaf.

Grated cheese and fried onion rings also make more substantial as well as tasty and attractive toppings and many of the Italian breads excel themselves in their rich variety of toppings – whole green or black olives, chunks of sun-dried tomatoes and roasted (bell) peppers are frequently added to ciabattas and focac-cias. As with glazes, toppings can also be added during and sometimes after cooking. Small breads, such as Vienna rolls, are baked until just golden, brushed with milk or cream and then strewn with sea salt, cumin or caraway seeds. They are then returned to the oven for a few more moments until cooked.

BELOW: For a dinner party or a buffet meal, bake a batch of rolls with assorted toppings.

BAKING TIMES

This will depend on the recipe, the size of the loaf and the heat of the oven. As a general rule, rolls take about 20 minutes, round country breads 40–50 minutes and tin loaves a little longer, 45–60 minutes. To check if bread is ready, remove it from the oven and tap firmly on the base of the loaf with your knuckles. It should have a hollow sound. If it seems soft or does not sound hollow, bake for a little longer.

ABOVE: Check rolls are ready by gently turning one over in a clean dish towel. The underside should be firm and golden, with no trace of moisture.

ABOVE: To check that a loaf is cooked, tap the base with your knuckles. It should be firm and sound hollow.

ADDING MOISTURE TO THE OVEN

A baker's oven is completely sealed and therefore produces the necessary steam for an evenly risen loaf. At home, glazing helps to produce steam, as does a tin of boiling water placed in the bottom of the oven, or you can spray water into the oven two or three times during cooking.

WHAT WENT WRONG

DOUGH WON'T RISE

You may have forgotten the yeast or the yeast may be past its "use-by" date and is dead. To save the dough, make up another batch, making certain the yeast is active. This dough can then be kneaded into the original dough. Alternatively, dissolve the new yeast in warm water and work it into the dough. Another time, always check that yeast is active before adding to flour.

SIDES AND BOTTOM OF BREAD ARE TOO PALE

The oven temperature was too low, or the tin (pan) did not allow heat to penetrate the crust. To remedy this, turn the loaf out of its tin and return it to the oven, placing it upside-down on a shelf, for 5–10 minutes.

CRUST TOO SOFT

There was insufficient steam in the oven. You could glaze the crusts before baking next time and spray the inside of the oven with water. Alternatively, place a little hot water in an ovenproof dish in the bottom of the oven during baking. This problem particularly besets French breads and other crusty loaves, which require a certain amount of steam in the oven.

CRUST TOO HARD

Using too much glaze or having too much steam in the oven can harden the crust, so use less glaze next time. To soften a crusty loaf, leave it overnight in a plastic bag.

CRUST SEPARATES FROM THE BREAD

This is caused either by the dough drying out during rising, or by the oven temperature being too low and the dough expanding unevenly. Next time, cover the dough with clear film (plastic wrap) or waxed paper to prevent any moisture loss while rising, and ensure that the oven is preheated to the correct temperature, so that heat penetrates uniformly.

SOFT PALE CRUST

This could be because the bread was not baked for long enough or perhaps the oven temperature was too low. When you think bread is ready, tap it firmly underneath; it should sound hollow. If it does not, return the bread to the oven, only this time placing it directly on the oven shelf.

LOAF IS CRUMBLY AND DRY

Either the bread was baked for too long or you used too much flour. Next time check the quantities in the recipe. It is also possible that the oven was too hot. Next time reduce the temperature and check the loaf when the crust looks golden brown.

LARGE HOLES IN LOAF

Either the dough was not knocked back (punched down) properly before shaping or it was not kneaded enough originally.

BREAD HAS A YEASTY FLAVOUR

Too much yeast was used. If doubling recipe quantities, do not double the amount of yeast but use one and a half times the amount. In addition, do not overcompensate for a cool room by adding extra yeast unless you don't mind a yeasty flavour. Wait a little longer instead – the bread will rise in the end.

LOAF COLLAPSES IN THE OVEN

Either the wrong flour was used for a particular recipe or the dough was left too long for the second rising and has over-risen. As a rule, the dough should only double in bulk.

LOAF IS DENSE AND FLAT

Too much liquid was used and the dough has become too soft, or was not kneaded enough. Always check the recipe for quantities of liquid needed until you are confident about judging the consistency of the dough. The dough should be kneaded firmly for at least 10 minutes.

BREAD-MAKING MACHINES

Bread makers may take the fun out of bread making, but if you enjoy home-made bread on a daily basis, they make it an incredibly easy process. All you need to do is add the correct ingredients, press the right buttons and – hey presto – a few hours later, you have a freshly cooked loaf of bread!

Many bread makers have a timer switch, so that you can programme your bread to be ready for when you get up in the morning. Almost all bread makers will make a variety of different types and sizes of loaves, and many have a feature where the bread maker does the kneading and rising, with the baking up to you – useful for French loaves, pizzas or any other breads that are not a standard loaf shape.

THINGS TO LOOK OUT FOR WHEN BUYING A BREAD-MAKING MACHINE

◆ Unless you are likely to need only one small loaf a day, choose a machine with the option of making small, medium and large loaves.
◆ Rapid or fast bake: this cuts down on the time taken to mix and bake a loaf. You will have a loaf in 1¾– 2 ¾ hours, although it will not be quite as large.
◆ Dough (or manual) cycle: allows you to remove the dough prior to shaping when making loaves that are not the standard "loaf" shape.
◆ Crust colour: bread makers have the option of dark, medium or pale crust.
◆ Sweet bread cycle: breads that are high in sugar or fat need to bake at slightly lower temperatures, other-wise these ingredients tend to burn. A sweet bread cycle can adjust the heat to allow for this.
◆ Timer feature: this useful feature allows you to set the bread maker so that the bread is ready for when you get up in the morning or when the children come home from school.
◆ Gluten free: A programme for mak-ing breads using gluten free flour and bread mixes.

USING A BREAD MAKER

1 Add the water, milk and/or other liquids to the bread pan (unless your manufacturers' instructions specify that the yeast is to go in first, in which case reverse the order in which you add the liquid and dry ingredients to the pan).

2 Add the flour, covering the liquid. Add salt, sugar and butter in separate corners, and the yeast in the centre. Place in the machine and select the programme.

3 Towards the end of the kneading process the machine will alert you to add any ingredients such as dried fruits, nuts, chocolate or olives, so they are not broken up by the kneading blade. Depending on the programme chosen your bread will be cooked within 1¾–5 hours.

TIPS FOR CONVERTING RECIPES

Once you're familiar with your bread machine and confident using suggested recipes, you will probably want to adapt some of your own favourite recipes. A loaf baked in a bread-making machine will, of course, always be "loaf-shaped", but since most bread makers have a dough cycle (where the dough is kneaded but not baked), it is possible to prepare rolls, ciabatta and baguettes – indeed most breads featured in this book. It is important that you reduce the recipe according to the max-imum capacity of your machine (and even further if you wish to make a small loaf).

Make sure that the proportions of all the essential ingredients for the recipe are approximately as follows:

FOR A SMALL LOAF
Flour: 375–400g/13–14oz/3¼–3¾ cups
Liquid (water/milk/eggs):
230–250ml/8–9fl oz/1–1 generous cup
Salt: 2.5–5ml/½ –1 tsp
Fat: 15–30g/1–2 tbsp
Sugar: 5–30ml/1 tsp–2 tbsp
Easy bake yeast: 3.5–5ml/ ¾–1 tsp

FOR A LARGE LOAF
Flour: 600–625g/21–22oz/5–5¼ cups
Liquid (water/milk/eggs): 370–420ml/
13–15fl oz/1½ cups +1 tbsp–1¾ cups
Salt: 5–7.5ml/1–1½ tsp
Fat: 15–60g/1–4 tbsp
Sugar: 10–45ml/2 tsp–3 tbsp
Easy bake yeast: 5–7.5ml/1–1½ tsp

◆ If adding fruit or other ingredients, reduce the quantities proportionately.
◆ Always use an easy bake or fast action dried yeast.
◆ If adding eggs, remember that one large egg is roughly equal to 60ml/4 tbsp liquid, so reduce the liquid accordingly.
◆ When adapting a recipe, monitor the machine carefully and make a note of any adjustments you may need to make. For instance, pay attention to whether the mixture is too moist or whether the machine struggles to knead the dough. If the loaf is too tall, this may be because you've added too much liquid, yeast or sugar, or added insufficient salt.

BREAD-MAKING EQUIPMENT

Bread making is not an exact science and you do not need a fully equipped kitchen with state-of-the-art utensils if you decide to have a go. In the long run, though, you may decide that some things are essential and others could be useful.

SCALES/WEIGHTS

Balance scales are more accurate but spring balance scales are easier to use and more convenient (especially if you have a tendency to lose the weights). Bear in mind, if buying scales for bread making, that you will probably be using large quantities of flours and will there-fore need large-size scales with a deep basin. Electronic scales are very useful as you can weigh the ingredients straight into the bowl and set the scales to zero as required.

BELOW: Be sure to get scales with a large measuring bowl.

LEFT: Sieves for flour or spices

MEASURING JUGS (CUPS)

Heatproof glass jugs are most convenient as liquids can safely be heated in them in the microwave and they are dishwasher safe. Measurements should be clearly marked on the outside; be sure to buy jugs with both imperial and metric measurements so that you can follow any recipe with ease.

MEASURING SPOONS

These are always useful in the kitchen for adding small quan-tities of spices etc. A set of spoons measures from 1.5ml/¼ tsp to 15ml/1 tbsp.

FOOD PROCESSOR

Most food processors can mix and knead dough efficiently in a fraction of the time it takes by hand. Check the instruction book about bread making since only the larger machines can handle large amounts of dough; it may be necessary to knead the dough in batches.

FOOD MIXER

An electric mixer fitted with a dough hook will knead dough in a time similar kneading by hand but with much less effort. Small machines can cope with only small amounts of dough and if you are considering buying a machine for bread-mak-ing, make sure that the equipment is suitable for the quantities of bread you will make.

SIEVES

Some finer breads may require the flour to be sifted so it is worth having at least one large sieve for flours and a smaller sieve for adding ground spices or dusting the loaves with flour or icing (confectioners') sugar after baking them.

ABOVE: A selection of glass bowls

BOWLS

If you have not got a selection already, it is worth buying some now since it is not possible to make bread (at least in the kitchen) without at least two good-sized bowls. Choose a bowl with a wide mouth, which is still deep enough to contain the batter or dough. A smaller bowl is also useful (although you can use the measuring jug or cup) for making up dried yeast.

ROLLING PIN

Some doughs need to be rolled out and you will need a large rolling pin for this job. A wooden rolling pin that is long and smooth and has no separate handles is ideal for bread making.

DOUGH KNIFE OR SCRAPER

This is extremely handy when kneading dough by hand. The rectangular piece of steel on a wooden handle is particularly useful in the early part of kneading, for lifting and working sticky or difficult doughs. The blades normally measure about 10 × 13cm/4 × 5in and should ideally be slightly flexible rather than rigid.

COOK'S KNIFE

You will need a sharp knife for slashing the dough – either during rising or just before baking. Some recipe books suggest using a razor for this job but the blade does need to be very sharp indeed. Since a good cook's knife can be kept in razor-sharp condition, this is the preferable option and adds a professional touch to your loaves.

ABOVE: Bread knife and cook's knife

LEFT: Dough knife/scraper

ABOVE: Rolling pin

ABOVE: Pastry brushes

BREAD KNIFE

A dull knife can wreak havoc on a fresh loaf of bread, so make sure you use a good bread knife. Bread should be cut in a sawing motion, which is why bread knives have long serrated blades. A plain cook's knife, although it will cut through the bread, will spoil the texture of the crumb.

PASTRY BRUSH

This is essential for glazing loaves and rolls. Choose a good, wide brush. It is worth spending extra for a brush that will not lose its bristles. Use a brush made from natural fibres; nylon will melt if used for brushing hot loaves during cooking.

BREAD TINS

Bread tins (pans) come in all sizes and it is worth having a selection. Include a 450g/1lb and preferably two 1kg/2¼ lb tins so that you can make loaves in a variety of shapes and sizes. If the tins are labelled with their dimensions, rather than their capacity, look out for 18 × 7.5cm/7 × 3in (equivalent to 450g/1lb) and 23 × 13cm/9 × 5in (equivalent to 1kg/2¼ lb). Other useful sizes are 30 × 10cm/12 × 4in and 25 × 10cm/10 × 4in. Professional bakers prefer matt black tins, which absorb the heat better than the shiny ones and therefore make the crust crisper. The wider

BELOW: Shallow loaf and cake tins

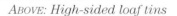
ABOVE: High-sided loaf tins

shallow tins are mostly used for fruit breads. Tin loaves are baked in plain, high-sided tins; farmhouse loaves are slightly shallower and tins may be stamped with the word "Farmhouse". Cake tins (pans) are sometimes used for bread making. Monkey bread, for instance, is baked in a 23cm/9in springform ring cake tin, while buchty – breakfast rolls that are batch-baked – require a square, loose-bottomed cake tin with straight sides that will support the rolls as they rise.

Several speciality breads are baked in a deep 15cm/6in cake tin. These breads include *panettone* and Sally Lunn.

If you are fond of baking focaccia, you will find a 25cm/10in pizza pan or shallow round cake tin invaluable.

MOULDS

There are various sizes of brioche mould for the traditional fluted brioche, including individual bun size. A *kugelhopf* mould is a fluted ring mould essential for making the Alsace or German *kugel-hopf* or the Viennese *gugelhupf*. A savarin mould is a straight-sided ring mould for

savarins and other ring-shaped breads. If you don't have the correct mould, it is sometimes possible to improvise. Boston brown bread, for instance, can be baked in a special mould, but the heatproof glass jar from a cafetière coffee jug (carafe) can be used instead, or even two 450g/1lb coffee cans, without the lids, work perfectly well once washed and dried.

BELOW: Baking sheets and patty tins

BAKING SHEETS
When buying baking sheets, look for ones that are either completely flat, or have a lip only on one long edge. This makes it easier to slide bread or rolls on to a wire rack. Strong, heavy baking sheets distribute the heat evenly.

MUFFIN TINS AND PATTY TINS
Muffin tins (pans) with 7.5cm/3in cups are very useful for making elaborately shaped rolls like the aptly named New England Fantans, while the larger patty tins and

Yorkshire pudding tins come into their own for specialities like Georgian Khachapuri. The tins support the dough while it is filled with cheese and then tied into a topknot.

FLOWER POTS
Earthenware flower pots can also be used for baking. These need to be tempered before being used for bread. Brush the

new, perfectly clean pots liberally inside and out with oil and place in a hot oven (about 200°C/400°F/Gas 6) for about 30 minutes. (This can conveniently be done while you are cooking something else.) Do this several times until the pots are impregnated with oil. They can then be used for baking bread and will need very little greasing.

BELOW: Earthenware flower pots make unusual moulds for loaves.

LEFT: A French fluted brioche mould and a savarin or ring mould

BREAD RECIPES OF THE WORLD

There are few things more pleasurable than the aroma and taste of freshly cooked home-made bread. This collection of recipes includes savoury and sweet classics from around the world, as well as a good selection of lesser-known specialities. A wide variety of flours, all of which are readily available, has been used to create distinctive breads which reflect the different flavours of the regions. These recipes aim to take the mystery out of bread-making and inspire you to try baking many different and delicious breads.

BRITISH BREADS

The range of British breads is extensive and includes a variety of shapes with picturesque names, including the bloomer, cob, split tin and cottage loaf. The textures and tastes are influenced by different ingredients and cooking methods. Welsh clay pot loaves, as their name suggests, are baked in clay flower pots and flavoured with herbs and garlic, while in Scotland, where bannocks and oatcakes are cooked on a girdle or griddle, grains such as barley and oatmeal contribute to the country-fresh flavours. Doughs enriched with dried fruits, such as Welsh bara brith and Cornish saffron bread, are delicious regional specialities.

GRANARY COB

450g/1lb/4 cups Granary (whole-
wheat) or malthouse flour
10ml/2 tsp salt
15g/½ oz fresh yeast
300ml/½ pint/1¼ cups lukewarm
water or milk and water mixed

FOR THE TOPPING
30ml/2 tbsp water
2.5ml/½ tsp salt
wheat flakes or cracked wheat,
to sprinkle

MAKES 1 ROUND LOAF

Cob is an old word meaning "head". If you make a slash across the top of the
dough, the finished loaf, known as a Danish cob, will look like a large roll.
A Coburg cob has a cross cut in the top before baking.

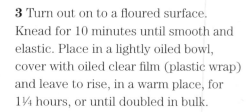

1 Lightly flour a baking sheet. Sift the flour and salt together in a large bowl and make a well in the centre. Place in a very low oven for 5 minutes to warm.

2 Mix the yeast with a little of the water or milk mixture then blend in the rest. Add the yeast mixture to the centre of the flour and mix to a dough.

3 Turn out on to a floured surface. Knead for 10 minutes until smooth and elastic. Place in a lightly oiled bowl, cover with oiled clear film (plastic wrap) and leave to rise, in a warm place, for 1¼ hours, or until doubled in bulk.

4 Turn the dough out on to a lightly floured surface and knock back (punch down). Knead for 2–3 minutes, then roll into a ball, making sure the dough looks like a plump round cushion, otherwise it will become too flat. Place in the centre of the prepared baking sheet. Cover with an inverted bowl and leave to rise, in a warm place, for 30–45 minutes.

5 Mix the water and salt and brush over the bread. Sprinkle with wheat flakes or cracked wheat.

6 Meanwhile, preheat the oven to 230°C/450°F/Gas 8. Bake for 15 minutes, then reduce the oven temperature to 200°C/400°F/Gas 6 and bake for a further 20 minutes, or until the loaf is firm to the touch and sounds hollow when tapped on the base. Cool on a wire rack.

Per loaf Energy 1395kcal/5931kJ; Protein 57.1g; Carbohydrate 287.6g, of which sugars 9.4g; Fat 9.9g, of which saturates 1.4g; Cholesterol 0mg; Calcium 172mg; Fibre 40.5g; Sodium 4926mg.

CHEESE AND ONION LOAF

Almost a meal in itself, this hearty bread tastes delicious as an accompaniment to salads and cold meats, or with soup.

1 Lightly grease a 25 × 10cm/10 × 4in loaf tin (pan). Melt 25g/1oz/2 tbsp of the butter in a heavy frying pan and sauté the onion until it is soft and light golden. Set aside to cool.

2 Sift the flour into a large bowl and stir in the yeast, mustard, salt and pepper. Stir in three-quarters of the grated cheese and the onion. Make a well in the centre. Add the milk and water; blend to a soft dough. Turn out on to a lightly floured surface and knead for 10 minutes until smooth and elastic.

3 Place the dough in a lightly oiled bowl, cover with oiled clear film (plastic wrap) and leave in a warm place, for about 45–60 minutes, until doubled in bulk.

4 Turn the dough out on to a lightly floured surface, knock back (punch down), and knead gently. Divide into 20 equal pieces and shape into small rounds. Place half in the prepared tin and brush with some melted butter. Top with the remaining rounds of dough and brush with the remaining butter.

5 Cover with oiled clear film and leave to rise for 45 minutes, until the dough reaches the top of the tin. Meanwhile, preheat the oven to 190°C/375°F/Gas 5.

6 Sprinkle the remaining cheese over the top. Bake for 40–45 minutes or until risen and golden brown. Cool on a wire rack.

1 onion, finely chopped
45g/1¾oz/3½ tbsp butter
450g/1lb/4 cups unbleached white bread flour
7g/¼oz sachet easy bake (rapid-rise) dried yeast
5ml/1 tsp mustard powder
175g/6oz/1½ cups grated mature (sharp) Cheddar cheese
150ml/¼ pint/⅔ cup lukewarm milk
150ml/¼ pint/⅔ cup lukewarm water
salt and ground black pepper

MAKES 1 LARGE LOAF

COOK'S TIP
If you prefer, use 20g/¾ oz fresh yeast instead of the easy bake yeast. Mix the fresh yeast with the milk until dissolved, then add to the flour.

Per loaf Energy 2707kcal/11384kJ; Protein 94.1g; Carbohydrate 363.1g, of which sugars 17.8g; Fat 104.8g, of which saturates 64.7g; Cholesterol 282mg; Calcium 2142mg; Fibre 14.8g; Sodium 1701mg.

POPPY-SEEDED BLOOMER

This satisfying white bread, which is the British version of the chunky baton loaf found throughout Europe, is made by a slower rising method and with less yeast than usual. It produces a longer-keeping loaf with a fuller flavour. The dough takes about 8 hours to rise, so you'll need to start this bread early in the morning.

675g/1½ lb/6 cups unbleached white bread flour
10ml/2 tsp salt
15g/½ oz fresh yeast
430ml/15fl oz/1⅞ cups water

FOR THE TOPPING
2.5ml/½ tsp salt
30ml/2 tbsp water
poppy seeds, for sprinkling

MAKES 1 LARGE LOAF

1 Lightly grease a baking sheet. Sift the flour and salt together into a large bowl and make a well in the centre.

2 Mix the yeast and 150ml/¼ pint/⅔ cup of the water in a jug (pitcher) or bowl. Mix in the remaining water. Add to the centre of the flour. Mix, gradually incorporating the surrounding flour, until the mixture forms a firm dough.

COOK'S TIP
The traditional cracked, crusty appearance of this loaf is difficult to achieve in a domestic oven. However, you can get a similar result by spraying the oven with water before baking. If the underneath of the loaf is not very crusty at the end of baking, turn the loaf over on the baking sheet, switch off the heat and leave in the oven for a further 5–10 minutes.

VARIATION
For a more rustic loaf, replace up to half the flour with wholemeal (whole-wheat) bread flour.

3 Turn out on to a lightly floured surface and knead the dough very well, for at least 10 minutes, until smooth and elastic. Place in a lightly oiled bowl, cover with lightly oiled clear film (plastic wrap) and leave at cool room temperature, about 15–18°C/60–65°F, for 5–6 hours, or until doubled in bulk.

4 Knock back (punch down) the dough, turn out on to a lightly floured surface and knead it thoroughly and quite hard for about 5 minutes. Return the dough to the bowl, and re-cover. Leave to rise, at cool room temperature, for a further 2 hours or slightly longer.

5 Knock back again and repeat the thorough kneading. Leave the dough to rest for 5 minutes, then roll out on a lightly floured surface into a rectangle 2.5cm/1in thick. Roll the dough up from one long side and shape it into a square-ended thick baton shape about 33 × 13cm/13 × 5in.

6 Place it seam side up on a lightly floured baking sheet, cover and leave to rest for 15 minutes. Turn the loaf over and place on the greased baking sheet. Plump up by tucking the dough under the sides and ends. Using a sharp knife, cut 6 diagonal slashes on the top.

7 Leave to rest, covered, in a warm place, for 10 minutes. Meanwhile preheat the oven to 230°C/450°F/Gas 8.

8 Mix the salt and water together and brush this glaze over the bread. Sprinkle with poppy seeds.

9 Spray the oven with water, bake the bread immediately for 20 minutes, then reduce the oven temperature to 200°C/400°F/Gas 6; bake for 25 minutes more, or until golden. Transfer to a wire rack to cool.

COTTAGE LOAF

*675g/1½ lb/6 cups unbleached white
bread flour
10ml/2 tsp salt
20g/¾ oz fresh yeast
400ml/14fl oz/1⅔ cups lukewarm
water*

MAKES 1 LARGE ROUND LOAF

COOK'S TIPS
• To ensure a good-shaped cottage loaf
the dough needs to be firm enough to
support the weight of the top ball.
• Do not over-prove the dough on
the second rising or the loaf may
topple over – but even if it does it will
still taste good.

*Snipping the top and bottom sections of the dough at 5cm/2in intervals not
only looks good but also helps the loaf to expand in the oven.*

1 Lightly grease two baking sheets. Sift
the flour and salt together into a large
bowl and make a well in the centre.

2 Mix the yeast in 150ml/¼ pint/⅔ cup
of the water until dissolved. Pour into
the centre of the flour with the
remaining water and mix to a firm dough.

3 Knead on a lightly floured surface for
10 minutes until smooth and elastic.
Place in a lightly oiled bowl, cover with
lightly oiled clear film (plastic wrap) and
leave to rise, in a warm place, for about
1 hour, or until doubled in bulk.

4 Turn out on to a lightly floured surface
and knock back (punch down). Knead
for 2–3 minutes then divide into two-
thirds and one-third; shape each to a ball.

5 Place the balls of dough on the prepared
baking sheets. Cover with inverted bowls
and leave to rise, in a warm place, for
about 30 minutes (see Cook's Tips).

6 Gently flatten the top of the larger
round of dough and, with a sharp knife,
cut a cross in the centre, about 4cm/
1½ in across. Brush with a little water
and place the smaller round on top.

7 Carefully press a hole through the
middle of the top ball, down into the
lower part, using your thumb and first
two fingers of one hand. Cover with
lightly oiled clear film and leave to rest
in a warm place for about 10 minutes.
Preheat the oven to 220°C/ 425°F/Gas 7
and place the bread on the lower shelf.
It will finish expanding as the oven heats
up. Bake for 35–40 minutes, or until
golden brown and sounding hollow
when tapped. Cool on a wire rack.

Per loaf Energy 2302kcal/9794kJ; Protein 77.6g; Carbohydrate 508.3g, of which sugars 9.4g; Fat 9.4g, of which saturates 1.4g; Cholesterol 0mg; Calcium 946mg; Fibre 20.9g; Sodium 3950mg.

WELSH CLAY POT LOAVES

*These breads are flavoured with chives, sage, parsley and garlic. You can use
any selection of your favourite herbs. For even more flavour, try adding a
little grated raw onion and grated cheese to the dough.*

*115g/4oz/1 cup wholemeal
(whole-wheat) bread flour
350g/12oz/3 cups unbleached white
bread flour
7.5ml/1½ tsp salt
15g/½ oz fresh yeast
150ml/¼ pint/⅔ cup lukewarm milk
120ml/4fl oz/½ cup lukewarm water
50g/2oz/4 tbsp butter, melted
15ml/1 tbsp chopped fresh chives
15ml/1 tbsp chopped fresh parsley
5ml/1 tsp chopped fresh sage
1 garlic clove, crushed
beaten egg, for glazing
fennel seeds, for sprinkling (optional)*

MAKES 2 LOAVES

COOK'S TIP
To prepare and seal new clay flower
pots, clean them thoroughly, oil them
inside and outside and bake them
three or four times. Preheat the oven
to about 200°C/400°F/Gas 6 and bake
for 30–40 minutes. Try to do this
while you are baking other foods.

1 Lightly grease 2 clean 14cm/5½ in
diameter, 11cm/4½ in high clay flower
pots. Sift the flours and salt together
into a large bowl and make a well in the
centre. Blend the yeast with a little of
the milk until smooth, then stir in the
remaining milk. Pour the yeast liquid
into the centre of the flour and sprinkle
over a little of the flour from around the
edge. Cover the bowl and leave in a
warm place for 15 minutes.

2 Add the water, melted butter, herbs
and garlic to the flour mixture and blend
together to form a dough. Turn out on to
a lightly floured surface and knead for
about 10 minutes until the dough is
smooth and elastic.

3 Place in a lightly oiled bowl, cover
with lightly oiled clear film (plastic
wrap) and leave in a warm place, for
1¼–1½ hours, or until doubled in bulk.

4 Turn the dough out on to a lightly floured
surface and knock back (punch down).
Divide in two. Shape and fit into the
prepared flower pots. They should about
half fill the pots. Cover with oiled clear
film and leave to rise for 30–45 minutes,
in a warm place, or until the dough is
2.5cm/1in from the top of the pots.

5 Meanwhile, preheat the oven to 200°C/
400°F/Gas 6. Brush the tops with
beaten egg and sprinkle with fennel
seeds, if using. Bake for 35–40 minutes
or until golden. Turn out on to a wire
rack to cool.

Per loaf Energy 1005kcal/4245kJ; Protein 27.3g; Carbohydrate 177.6g, of which sugars 8.2g; Fat 25.6g, of which saturates 14.8g; Cholesterol 62mg; Calcium 412mg; Fibre 12g; Sodium 1718mg.

SPLIT TIN

500g/1¼ lb/5 cups unbleached white bread flour, plus extra for dusting
10ml/2 tsp salt
15g/½ oz fresh yeast
300ml/½ pint/1¼ cups lukewarm water
60ml/4 tbsp lukewarm milk

MAKES 1 LOAF

As its name suggests, this homely loaf is so called because of the centre split. Some bakers mould the dough in two loaves – they join together whilst proving but retain the characteristic crack after baking.

1 Lightly grease a 900g/2lb loaf tin (pan) (18.5 × 11.5cm/7¼ × 4½in). Sift the flour and salt together into a large bowl and make a well in the centre. Mix the yeast with half the lukewarm water in a jug (pitcher), then stir in the remaining water.

2 Pour the yeast mixture into the centre of the flour and using your fingers, mix in a little flour. Gradually mix in more of the flour from around the edge of the bowl to form a thick, smooth batter.

3 Sprinkle a little more flour from around the edge over the batter and leave in a warm place to "sponge". Bubbles will appear in the batter after about 20 minutes. Add the milk and remaining flour; mix to a firm dough.

4 Place on a lightly floured surface and knead for about 10 minutes until smooth and elastic. Place in a lightly oiled bowl, cover with oiled clear film (plastic wrap) and leave in a warm place, for 1–1¼ hours, or until nearly doubled in bulk.

5 Knock back (punch down) the dough and turn out on to a lightly floured surface. Shape it into a rectangle, the length of the tin. Roll up lengthways, tuck the ends under and place seam side down in the prepared tin. Cover and leave to rise, in a warm place, for about 20–30 minutes, or until nearly doubled in bulk.

6 Using a sharp knife, make one deep central slash the length of the bread; dust with flour. Leave for 10–15 minutes.

7 Meanwhile, preheat the oven to 230°C/450°F/Gas 8. Bake for 15 minutes, then reduce the oven temperature to 200°C/400°F/Gas 6. Bake for 20–25 minutes more, or until the bread is golden and sounds hollow when tapped on the base. Turn out on to a wire rack to cool.

Per loaf Energy 1733kcal/7367kJ; Protein 49g; Carbohydrate 391.5g, of which sugars 10.5g; Fat 7.5g, of which saturates 1.6g; Cholesterol 4mg; Calcium 773mg; Fibre 15.5g; Sodium 3978mg.

SHAPED DINNER ROLLS

These professional-looking rolls are perfect for entertaining. You can always make double the amount of dough and freeze half, tightly wrapped. Just thaw, glaze and bake as required.

450g/1lb/4 cups unbleached white bread flour
10ml/2 tsp salt
2.5ml/½ tsp caster (superfine) sugar
7g/¼oz sachet easy bake (rapid-rise) dried yeast
50g/2oz/¼ cup butter or margarine
250ml/8fl oz/1 cup lukewarm milk
1 egg

FOR THE TOPPING
1 egg yolk
15ml/1 tbsp water
poppy seeds and sesame seeds

MAKES 12 ROLLS

1 Lightly grease two baking sheets. Sift the flour and salt into a large bowl and stir in the sugar and yeast. Add the butter or margarine and rub in until the mixture resembles fine breadcrumbs.

2 Make a well in the centre. Add the milk and egg to the well and mix to a dough. Knead on a floured surface for 10 minutes until smooth and elastic. Place in a lightly oiled bowl, cover with lightly oiled clear film (plastic wrap) and leave to rise, in a warm place, for 1 hour, or until doubled in bulk.

3 Turn the dough out on to a lightly floured surface, knock back (punch down) and knead for 2–3 minutes. Divide the dough into 12 equal pieces and shape into rolls as described in steps 4–8.

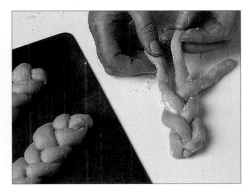

4 *To make braids:* divide each piece of dough into three equal pieces. Working on a lightly floured surface, roll each piece to a sausage, keeping the lengths and widths even. Pinch three strips together at one end, then braid them neatly but not too tightly. Pinch the ends together and tuck under the braid.

5 *To make trefoils:* divide each piece of dough into three and roll into balls. Place the three balls together in a triangular shape.

6 *To make batons:* shape each piece of dough into an oblong and slash the surface of each with diagonal cuts just before baking.

7 *To make cottage rolls:* divide each piece of dough into two-thirds and one-third and shape into rounds. Place the small one on top of the large one and make a hole through the centre with the handle of a wooden spoon.

8 *To make knots:* shape each piece of dough into a long roll and tie a single knot, pulling the ends through.

9 Place the dinner rolls on the prepared baking sheets, spacing them well apart, cover the rolls with oiled clear film and leave to rise, in a warm place, for about 30 minutes, or until doubled in bulk.

10 Meanwhile, preheat the oven to 220°C/425°F/Gas 7. Mix the egg yolk and water together for the glaze and brush over the rolls. Sprinkle some with poppy seeds and some with sesame seeds. Bake for 15–18 minutes or until golden. Lift the rolls off the sheet using a metal spatula and transfer to a wire rack to cool.

Per roll Energy 195kcal/822kJ; Protein 5.5g; Carbohydrate 30.4g, of which sugars 1.8g; Fat 6.6g, of which saturates 3g; Cholesterol 43mg; Calcium 99mg; Fibre 1.4g; Sodium 378mg.

CRUMPETS

Home-made crumpets are less doughy and not as heavy as most supermarket versions. Serve them lightly toasted, oozing with butter.

225g/8oz/2 cups unbleached plain (all-purpose) flour
225g/8oz/2 cups unbleached white bread flour
10ml/2 tsp salt
600ml/1 pint/2½ cups milk and water mixed
30ml/2 tbsp sunflower oil
15ml/1 tbsp caster (superfine) sugar
15g/½ oz fresh yeast
2.5ml/½ tsp bicarbonate of soda (baking soda)
120ml/4fl oz/½ cup lukewarm water

MAKES ABOUT 20 CRUMPETS

1 Lightly grease a griddle or heavy frying pan and 4 × 8cm/3¼ in plain pastry (cookie) cutters or crumpet rings.

2 Sift the flours and salt together into a large bowl and make a well in the centre. Heat the milk and water mixture, oil and sugar until lukewarm. Mix the yeast with 150ml/¼ pint/⅔ cup of this liquid.

3 Add the yeast mixture and remaining liquid to the centre of the flour and beat vigorously for about 5 minutes until smooth and elastic. Cover with oiled clear film (plastic wrap) and leave in a warm place, for about 1½ hours, or until the mixture is bubbly and about to fall.

4 Dissolve the soda in the lukewarm water and stir into the batter. Re-cover and leave to rise for 30 minutes.

5 Place the cutters or crumpet rings on the griddle and warm over a medium heat. Fill the cutters or rings a generous 1cm/½ in deep. Cook over a gentle heat for 6–7 minutes. The tops should be dry, with a mass of tiny holes.

6 Carefully remove the cutters or rings and turn the crumpets over. Cook for 1–2 minutes or until pale golden. Repeat with remaining batter. Serve warm.

ENGLISH MUFFINS

Perfect served warm, split open and buttered for afternoon tea; or try these favourites toasted, split and topped with ham and eggs for brunch.

450g/1lb/4 cups unbleached white bread flour
7.5ml/1½ tsp salt
350–375ml/12–13fl oz/1½–1⅔ cups lukewarm milk
2.5ml/½ tsp caster (superfine) sugar
15g/½oz fresh yeast
15ml/1 tbsp melted butter or olive oil
rice flour or semolina, for dusting

MAKES 9 MUFFINS

1 Generously flour a non-stick baking sheet. Very lightly grease a griddle. Sift the flour and salt together into a large bowl and make a well in the centre. Blend 150ml/¼ pint/⅔ cup of the milk, sugar and yeast together. Stir in the remaining milk and butter or oil.

2 Add the yeast mixture to the centre of the flour and beat for 4–5 minutes until smooth and elastic. The dough will be soft but just hold its shape. Cover with lightly oiled clear film (plastic wrap) and leave to rise, in a warm place, for 45–60 minutes, or until doubled in bulk.

3 Turn out on a floured surface and knock back (punch down). Roll out to 1cm/½ in thick. Using a floured 7.5cm/3in plain cutter, cut out nine rounds.

4 Dust with rice flour or semolina and place on the prepared baking sheet. Cover and leave to rise, in a warm place, for about 20–30 minutes.

5 Warm the griddle over a medium heat. Carefully transfer the muffins in batches to the griddle. Cook slowly for about 7 minutes on each side or until golden brown. Transfer to a wire rack to cool.

LARDY CAKE

450g/1lb/4 cups unbleached white bread flour
5ml/1 tsp salt
15g/½ oz/1 tbsp lard (shortening)
25g/1oz/2 tbsp caster (superfine) sugar
20g/¾ oz fresh yeast
300ml/½ pint/1¼ cups lukewarm water

FOR THE FILLING
75g/3oz/6 tbsp lard (shortening)
75g/3oz/6 tbsp soft light brown sugar
115g/4oz/½ cup currants,
slightly warmed
75g/3oz/½ cup sultanas (golden raisins), slightly warmed
25g/1oz/3 tbsp mixed chopped (candied) peel
5ml/1 tsp mixed (apple pie) spice

FOR THE GLAZE
10ml/2 tsp sunflower oil
15–30ml/1–2 tbsp caster (superfine) sugar

MAKES 1 LARGE LOAF

This special rich fruit bread was originally made throughout many counties of England for celebrating the harvest. Using lard rather than butter or margarine makes an authentic lardy cake.

1 Grease a 25 × 20cm/10 × 8in shallow roasting pan. Sift the flour and salt into a large bowl and rub in the lard. Stir in the sugar and make a well in the centre.

2 In a bowl, cream the yeast with half of the water, then blend in the remainder. Add to the centre of the flour and mix to a smooth dough.

3 Turn out on to a lightly floured surface and knead for 10 minutes until smooth and elastic. Place in a lightly oiled bowl, cover with oiled clear film (plastic wrap) and leave in a warm place, for 1 hour, or until doubled in bulk.

4 Turn the dough out on to a lightly floured surface and knock back (punch down). Knead for 2–3 minutes. Roll into a rectangle about 5mm/¼ in thick.

5 Using half the lard for the filling, cover the top two-thirds of the dough with flakes of lard. Sprinkle over half the sugar, half the dried fruits and peel and half the mixed spice. Fold the bottom third up and the top third down, sealing the edges with the rolling pin.

6 Turn the dough by 90 degrees. Repeat the rolling and cover with the remaining lard, fruit and peel and mixed spice. Fold, seal and turn as before. Roll out the dough to fit the prepared pan. Cover with lightly oiled clear film and leave to rise, in a warm place, for 30–45 minutes, or until doubled in size.

7 Meanwhile, preheat the oven to 200°C/400°F/Gas 6. Brush the top of the lardy cake with sunflower oil and sprinkle with caster sugar.

8 Score a criss-cross pattern on top using a sharp knife, then bake for 30–40 minutes until golden. Turn out on to a wire rack to cool slightly. Serve warm, cut into slices or squares.

Per loaf Energy 3499kcal/14750kJ; Protein 47.5g; Carbohydrate 598.9g, of which sugars 256g; Fat 117.9g, of which saturates 40.7g; Cholesterol 84mg; Calcium 872mg; Fibre 18.8g; Sodium 2087mg.

CORNISH SAFFRON BREADS

Often called saffron cake, this light, delicately spiced bread contains threads of saffron and is made in a loaf tin. Whatever the name, the flavour and texture are superb.

300ml/½ pint/1¼ cups milk
2.5ml/½ tsp saffron threads
400g/14oz/3½ cups unbleached white bread flour
25g/1oz fresh yeast
50g/2oz/½ cup ground almonds
2.5ml/½ tsp grated nutmeg
2.5ml/½ tsp ground cinnamon
50g/2oz/¼ cup caster (superfine) sugar
2.5ml/½ tsp salt
75g/3oz/6 tbsp butter, softened
50g/2oz/⅓ cup sultanas (golden raisins)
50g/2oz/¼ cup currants

FOR THE GLAZE
30ml/2 tbsp milk
15ml/1 tbsp caster (superfine) sugar

MAKES 2 LOAVES

1 Grease two 900g/2lb loaf tins (pans). Heat half the milk until almost boiling.

2 Place the saffron threads in a small heatproof bowl and pour over the milk. Stir gently, then leave to infuse (steep) for 30 minutes.

3 Heat the remaining milk in the same pan until it is just lukewarm.

4 Place 50g/2oz/½ cup flour in a small bowl, crumble in the yeast and stir in the lukewarm milk. Mix well, then leave for about 15 minutes until the yeast starts to ferment.

5 Mix the remaining flour, ground almonds, spices, sugar and salt together in a large bowl and make a well in the centre. Add the saffron infusion, yeast mixture and softened butter to the centre of the flour and mix to a very soft dough.

6 Turn out on to a lightly floured surface and knead for 5 minutes until smooth and elastic. Place in a lightly oiled bowl, cover with lightly oiled clear (plastic wrap) film and leave in a warm place, for 1½–2 hours, or until doubled in bulk.

7 Turn the dough out on to a lightly floured surface, knock back (punch down), and knead in the sultanas and currants. Divide in two and shape into two loaves. Place in the prepared tins. Cover with oiled clear film and leave to rise, in a warm place, for 1½ hours, or until the dough reaches the top of the tins.

8 Meanwhile, preheat the oven to 220°C/425°F/Gas 7. Bake the loaves for 10 minutes, then reduce the oven temperature to 190°C/375°F/Gas 5 and bake for 15–20 minutes or until golden.

9 While the loaves are baking, make the glaze. Heat the milk and sugar in a small pan, stirring until the sugar has dissolved. As soon as the loaves come out of the oven, brush them with the glaze, leave in the tins for 5 minutes, then turn out on to a wire rack to cool.

Per loaf Energy 1415kcal/5961kJ; Protein 30.6g; Carbohydrate 225.1g, of which sugars 72g; Fat 50g, of which saturates 23.3g; Cholesterol 95mg; Calcium 579mg; Fibre 9.1g; Sodium 875mg.

*115g/4oz/1 cup barley flour
50g/2oz/½ cup unbleached plain
(all-purpose) flour or wholemeal
(whole-wheat) flour
2.5ml/½ tsp salt
2.5ml/½ tsp cream of tartar
25g/1oz/2 tbsp butter or margarine
175ml/6fl oz/¾ cup buttermilk
2.5ml/½ tsp bicarbonate of soda
(baking soda)*

MAKES 1 ROUND LOAF

COOK'S TIPS
• If you cannot locate buttermilk,
then use soured milk instead. Stir
5ml/1 tsp lemon juice into
175ml/6 fl oz/¾ cup milk and set aside
for an hour to sour.
• If you find the earthy flavour of
barley flour too strong, reduce it to
50g/2oz/½ cup and increase the plain
white flour to 115g/4oz/1 cup.
Alternatively, replace half the barley
flour with fine oatmeal.

BARLEY BANNOCK

*Bannocks are flat loaves about the size of a dinner plate. They are
traditionally baked on a griddle or girdle (which is the preferred name in
Scotland). Barley flour adds a wonderfully earthy flavour to the bread.*

1 Wipe the surface of a griddle with a little vegetable oil. Sift the flours, salt and cream of tartar together into a large bowl. Add the butter or margarine and rub into the flour until it resembles fine breadcrumbs.

2 Mix the buttermilk and bicarbonate of soda together. When the mixture starts to bubble add to the flour. Mix together to form a soft dough. Do not over-mix the dough or it will toughen.

3 On a floured surface pat the dough out to form a round about 2cm/¾in thick. Mark the dough into four wedges, using a sharp knife, if you prefer.

4 Heat the griddle until hot. Cook the bannock on the griddle for about 8–10 minutes per side over a gentle heat. Do not cook too quickly or the outside will burn before the centre is cooked. Cool the bannock slightly on a wire rack and eat while still warm.

SCOTTISH OATCAKES

*115g/4oz/1 cup medium or
fine oatmeal
1.5ml/¼ tsp salt
pinch of bicarbonate of soda
(baking soda)
15ml/1 tbsp melted butter
or lard (shortening)
45–60ml/3–4 tbsp hot water*

MAKES 8 OATCAKES

VARIATIONS
• Oatcakes are traditionally cooked
on the griddle, but they can also
be cooked in the oven at 180°C/
350°F/Gas 4 for about 20 minutes, or
until pale golden in colour.
• Small round oatcakes can be
stamped out using a 7.5cm/3in plain
cutter, if preferred.

*The crunchy texture of these tempting oatcakes makes them difficult to resist.
Serve with butter and slices of a good cheese.*

1 Very lightly oil a griddle or heavy frying pan. Mix the oatmeal, salt and soda together in a bowl.

2 Add the melted butter or lard and sufficient hot water to make a dough. Lightly knead on a surface dusted with oatmeal until it is smooth. Cut the dough in half.

3 On an oatmeal-dusted surface roll each piece of dough out as thinly as possible into a round about 15cm/6in across and 5mm/¼in thick.

4 Cut each round into four quarters or farls. Heat the griddle over a medium heat until warm. Transfer four farls, using a spatula or fish slice, to the griddle and cook over a low heat for 4–5 minutes. The edges may start to curl.

5 Using the spatula or slice, carefully turn the farls over and cook for about 1–2 minutes. If preferred the second side can be cooked under a preheated grill (broiler) until crisp, but not brown. Transfer to a wire rack to cool. Repeat with the remaining farls.

WELSH BARA BRITH

This rich, fruity bread – the name literally means "speckled bread" – is a speciality from North Wales. The honey glaze makes a delicious topping.

20g/¾ oz fresh yeast
210ml/7fl oz/scant 1 cup lukewarm milk
450g/1lb/4 cups unbleached white bread flour
75g/3oz/6 tbsp butter or lard (shortening)
5ml/1 tsp mixed (apple pie) spice
2.5ml/½ tsp salt
50g/2oz/⅓ cup light brown sugar
1 egg, lightly beaten
115g/4oz/⅔ cup seedless raisins, slightly warmed
75g/3oz/scant ½ cup currants, slightly warmed
40g/1½ oz/¼ cup mixed chopped (candied) peel
15–30ml/1–2 tbsp clear honey, for glazing

MAKES 1 LARGE ROUND LOAF

1 Grease a baking sheet. Blend the yeast with a little of the milk, then stir in the remainder. Set aside for 10 minutes.

2 Sift the flour into a large bowl and rub in the butter or lard until the mixture resembles breadcrumbs. Stir in the mixed spice, salt and sugar and make a well in the centre.

3 Add the yeast mixture and beaten egg to the centre of the flour and mix to a rough dough.

4 Turn out the dough on to a lightly floured surface and knead for about 10 minutes until smooth and elastic. Place in a lightly oiled bowl, cover with lightly oiled clear film (plastic wrap) and leave to rise, in a warm place, for 1½ hours, or until doubled in bulk.

5 Turn out on to a lightly floured surface, knock back (punch down), and knead in the dried fruits and peel. Shape into a round and place on the baking sheet. Cover with oiled clear film and leave to rise, in a warm place, for 1 hour, or until the dough doubles in size.

6 Meanwhile, preheat the oven to 200°C/400°F/Gas 6. Bake for 30 minutes or until the bread sounds hollow when tapped on the base. If the bread starts to over-brown, cover it loosely with foil for the last 10 minutes. Transfer the bread to a wire rack, brush with honey and leave to cool.

VARIATIONS
• The bara brith can be baked in a 1.5–1.75 litre/2½–3 pint/6¼–7½ cup loaf tin (pan) or deep round or square cake tin (pan), if you prefer.
• For a more wholesome loaf, replace half the white flour with wholemeal (whole-wheat) bread flour.

Per loaf Energy 2729kcal/11566kJ; Protein 49.7g; Carbohydrate 557.8g, of which sugars 214.9g; Fat 48.7g, of which saturates 27.5g; Cholesterol 110mg; Calcium 890mg; Fibre 18.9g; Sodium 2414mg.

SALLY LUNN

*Sally Lunn is traditionally served warm sliced into three layers horizontally,
spread with clotted cream or butter and re-assembled. It looks fantastic.*

1 Lightly butter a 15cm/6in round cake tin (pan), 7.5cm/3in deep. Dust lightly with flour, if the tin lacks a non-stick finish. Melt the butter in a small pan and then stir in the milk or cream and sugar. The mixture should be tepid. Remove from the heat, add the yeast and blend thoroughly until the yeast has dissolved. Leave for 10 minutes, or until the yeast starts to work.

2 Sift the flour and salt together into a large bowl. Stir in the lemon rind and make a well in the centre. Add the yeast mixture to the centre of the flour and mix together to make a soft dough just stiff enough to form a shape.

3 Turn out the dough on to a lightly floured surface and knead for about 10 minutes until smooth and elastic. Shape into a ball and place in the prepared tin. Cover with lightly oiled clear film (plastic wrap) and leave in a warm place, for 1¼–1½ hours.

4 When the dough has risen almost to the top of the tin, remove the clear film.

5 Meanwhile, preheat the oven to 220°C/ 425°F/Gas 7. Bake for 15–20 minutes or until light golden. While the loaf is baking, heat the milk and sugar for the glaze in a small pan until the sugar has dissolved, then bring to the boil. Brush the glaze over the bread.

6 Leave to cool in the tin for 10 minutes, or until the bread comes away from the side easily, then cool slightly on a wire rack before slicing and filling.

*25g/1oz/2 tbsp butter
150ml/¼ pint/⅔ cup milk or
double (heavy) cream
15ml/1 tbsp caster (superfine) sugar
15g/½ oz fresh yeast
275g/10oz/2½ cups unbleached white
bread flour
2.5ml/½ tsp salt
finely grated rind of ½ lemon*

*FOR THE GLAZE
15ml/1 tbsp milk
15ml/1 tbsp caster (superfine) sugar*

MAKES 1 ROUND LOAF

Per loaf Energy 1250kcal/5290kJ; Protein 31g; Carbohydrate 236.9g, of which sugars 27.3g; Fat 26.6g, of which saturates 15.6g; Cholesterol 66mg; Calcium 577mg; Fibre 8.5g; Sodium 1262mg.

FRENCH BREADS

Although best known for the baguette, France has many more breads to offer, from specialities like decorative wheat-ear shaped epi or kugelhopf – which introduce nuts, onion and bacon – to rustic crusty breads like pain polka and that old-fashioned rye bread, pain bouillie. Enriched doughs are popular with the French and include the rich, buttery yet light classic breakfast treats of croissants and brioche. Perfect with a cup of coffee!

CROISSANTS

Golden layers of flaky pastry, puffy, light and flavoured with butter is how the best croissants should be. Serve warm on the day of baking.

350g/12oz/3 cups unbleached white bread flour
115g/4oz/1 cup fine French plain (all purpose) flour
5ml/1 tsp salt
25g/1oz/2 tbsp caster (superfine) sugar
15g/¹/₂ oz fresh yeast
225ml/scant 8fl oz/scant 1 cup lukewarm milk
1 egg, lightly beaten
225g/8oz/1 cup butter

For the Glaze
1 egg yolk
15ml/1 tbsp milk

Makes 14 Croissants

COOK'S TIP
Make sure that the block of butter and the dough are about the same temperature when combining, to ensure the best results.

1 Sift the flours and salt together into a large bowl. Stir in the sugar. Make a well in the centre. Cream the yeast with 45ml/3 tbsp of the milk, then stir in the remainder. Add the yeast mixture to the centre of the flour, then add the egg and gradually beat in the flour until it forms a dough.

2 Turn out on to a lightly floured surface and knead for 3–4 minutes. Place in a large lightly oiled bowl, cover with lightly oiled clear (plastic wrap) film and leave in a warm place, for about 45-60 minutes, or until doubled in bulk.

3 Knock back (punch down), re-cover and chill for 1 hour. Meanwhile, flatten the butter into a block about 2cm/³⁄₄in thick. Knock back the dough and turn out on to a lightly floured surface. Roll out into a rough 25cm/10in square, rolling the edges thinner than the centre.

4 Place the block of butter diagonally in the centre and fold the corners of the dough over the butter like an envelope, tucking in the edges to completely enclose the butter.

5 Roll the dough into a rectangle about 2cm/³⁄₄in thick, approximately twice as long as it is wide. Fold the bottom third up and the top third down and seal the edges with a rolling pin. Wrap in clear film and chill for 20 minutes.

6 Repeat the rolling, folding and chilling twice more, turning the dough by 90 degrees each time. Roll out on a floured surface into a 63 × 33cm/25 × 13in rectangle; trim the edges to leave a 60 × 30cm/24 × 12in rectangle. Cut in half lengthways. Cut crossways into 14 equal triangles with 15cm/6in bases.

7 Place the dough triangles on two baking sheets, cover with clear film and chill for 10 minutes.

8 To shape the croissants, place each one with the wide end at the top, hold each side and pull gently to stretch the top of the triangle a little, then roll towards the point, finishing with the pointed end tucked underneath. Curve the ends towards the pointed end to make a crescent. Place on two baking sheets, spaced well apart.

9 Mix together the egg yolk and milk for the glaze. Lightly brush a little glaze over the croissants, avoiding the cut edges of the dough. Cover the croissants loosely with lightly oiled clear film and leave to rise, in a warm place, for about 30 minutes, or until they are nearly doubled in size.

10 Meanwhile, preheat the oven to 220°C/425°F/Gas 7. Brush the croissants with the remaining glaze and bake for 15–20 minutes, or until crisp and golden. Transfer to a wire rack to cool slightly before serving warm.

VARIATION
To make chocolate-filled croissants, place a small square of milk or plain (semisweet) chocolate or 15ml/1 tbsp coarsely chopped chocolate at the wide end of each triangle before rolling up as in step 8.

Per croissant Energy 226kcal/943kJ; Protein 3.6g; Carbohydrate 25g, of which sugars 2.2g; Fat 13g, of which saturates 8.1g; Cholesterol 33mg; Calcium 71mg; Fibre 0.9g; Sodium 427mg.

PAIN BOUILLIE

This is an old-fashioned style of rye bread, made before sourdough starters were used. Rye flour is mixed with boiling water like a porridge and left overnight to ferment. The finished bread has a rich earthy flavour, with just a hint of caraway.

FOR THE PORRIDGE
225g/8oz/2 cups rye flour
450ml/¾ pint/1¾ cups boiling water
5ml/1 tsp clear honey

FOR THE DOUGH
7g/¼ oz fresh yeast
30ml/2 tbsp lukewarm water
5ml/1 tsp caraway seeds, crushed
10ml/2 tsp salt
350g/12oz/3 cups unbleached white bread flour
olive oil, for brushing

MAKES 2 LOAVES

1 Lightly grease a 23.5 × 13cm/9¼ × 5in loaf tin (pan). Place the rye flour for the porridge in a large bowl. Pour over the boiling water and leave to stand for 5 minutes. Stir in the honey. Cover with clear film (plastic wrap) and leave in a warm place for about 12 hours.

2 Make the dough. Put the yeast in a measuring jug (cup) and blend in the water. Stir the mixture into the porridge with the crushed caraway seeds and salt. Add the white flour a little at a time, mixing first with a wooden spoon and then with your hands, until the mixture forms a firm dough.

3 Turn out on to a lightly floured surface and knead for 6–8 minutes until smooth and elastic. Return to the bowl, cover with lightly oiled clear film (plastic wrap) and leave to rise, in a warm place, for 1½ hours, or until doubled in bulk.

4 Turn out on to a lightly floured surface and knock back (punch down). Cut into two equal pieces and roll each piece into a rectangle 38 × 12cm/15 × 4½in. Fold the bottom third up and the top third down and seal the edges. Turn over.

5 Brush one side of each piece of folded dough with olive oil and place side by side in the prepared tin, oiled edges next to each other. Cover with lightly oiled clear film and leave to rise, in a warm place, for 1 hour, or until the dough reaches the top of the tin.

6 Meanwhile, preheat the oven to 220°C/425°F/Gas 7. Brush the tops of the loaves with olive oil, and using a sharp knife, slash with one or two cuts. Bake for 30 minutes, then reduce the oven temperature to 190°C/375°F/Gas 5 and bake for a further 25–30 minutes. Turn out on to a wire rack to cool.

COOK'S TIP
Serve very thinly sliced, with a little butter, or as an accompaniment to cold meats and cheeses.

Per loaf Energy 996kcal/4235kJ; Protein 26.4g; Carbohydrate 225g, of which sugars 4.6g; Fat 5.2g, of which saturates 0.8g; Cholesterol 0mg; Calcium 291mg; Fibre 18.6g; Sodium 1974mg.

EPI

This pretty, wheat-ear shaped crusty loaf makes a good presentation bread. The recipe uses a piece of fermented French baguette dough as a starter, which improves the flavour and texture of the finished bread.

*7g/¼ oz fresh yeast
275ml/9fl oz/generous 1 cup
lukewarm water
115g/4oz/½ cup 6–10-hours-old
French baguette dough
225g/8oz/2 cups unbleached white
bread flour
75g/3oz/¾ cup fine French plain
(all-purpose) flour
5ml/1 tsp salt*

MAKES 2 LOAVES

COOK'S TIP
You can use any amount up to 10 per cent of previously made French baguette dough for this recipe. The épi can also be shaped into a circle to make an attractive crown.

5 Let the dough rest between rolling for a few minutes if necessary to avoid tearing. Pleat a floured dishtowel on a baking sheet to make two moulds for the loaves. Place them between the pleats of the towel, cover with lightly oiled clear film and leave to rise, in a warm place, for 30 minutes.

6 Meanwhile, preheat the oven to 230°C/450°F/Gas 8. Using scissors, make diagonal cuts halfway through the dough about 5cm/2in apart, alternating the cuts along the loaf. Gently pull the dough in the opposite direction.

7 Place on the prepared baking sheet and bake for 20 minutes, or until golden. Spray the inside of the oven with water 2–3 times during the first 5 minutes of baking. Transfer to a wire rack to cool.

1 Sprinkle a baking sheet with flour. Mix the yeast with the water in a jug (pitcher). Place the French bread dough in a large bowl and break up. Add a little of the yeast water to soften the dough. Mix in a little of the bread flour, then alternate the additions of yeast water and both flours until incorporated. Sprinkle the salt over the dough and knead in. Turn out the dough on to a lightly floured surface and knead for about 5 minutes until smooth and elastic.

2 Place in a lightly oiled bowl, cover with lightly oiled clear film (plastic wrap) and leave in a warm place, for about 1 hour, or until doubled in bulk.

3 Knock back the dough with your fist, then cover the bowl again with the oiled clear film and leave to rise, in a warm place, for about 1 hour.

4 Divide the dough into two equal pieces, place on a lightly floured surface and stretch each piece into a baguette.

Per loaf Energy 667kcal/2836kJ; Protein 19.6g; Carbohydrate 148.4g, of which sugars 3.4g; Fat 3.5g, of which saturates 0.7g; Cholesterol 0mg; Calcium 285mg; Fibre 5.5g; Sodium 1315mg.

PETITS PAINS AU LAIT

450g/1lb/4 cups unbleached white
bread flour
10ml/2 tsp salt
15ml/1 tbsp caster (superfine) sugar
50g/2oz/¼ cup butter, softened
15g/½ oz fresh yeast
280ml/9fl oz/generous 1 cup
lukewarm milk, plus 15ml/1 tbsp
extra milk, for glazing

MAKES 12 ROLLS

VARIATION
These can also be made into long rolls. To shape, flatten each ball of dough and fold in half. Roll back and forth, using your hand to form a 13cm/5in long roll, tapered at either end. Just before baking, slash the tops horizontally several times.

These classic French round milk rolls have a soft crust and a light, slightly sweet crumb. They won't last long!

1 Lightly grease two baking sheets. Sift the flour and salt together into a large bowl. Stir in the sugar. Rub the softened butter into the flour.

2 Cream the yeast with 60ml/4 tbsp of the milk. Stir in the remaining milk. Pour into the flour mixture and mix to a soft dough.

3 Turn out on to a lightly floured surface and knead for 8–10 minutes until smooth and elastic. Place in a lightly oiled bowl, cover with lightly oiled clear film (plastic wrap) and leave in a warm place, for 1 hour, or until doubled in bulk.

4 Turn out the dough on to a lightly floured surface and gently knock back (punch down). Divide into 12 equal pieces. Shape into balls and space on the baking sheets.

5 Using a sharp knife, cut a cross in the top of each roll. Cover with lightly oiled clear film and leave to rise, in a warm place, for about 20 minutes, or until doubled in size.

6 Preheat the oven to 200°C/400°F/ Gas 6. Brush the rolls with milk and bake for 20–25 minutes, or until golden. Transfer to a wire rack to cool.

FRENCH DIMPLED ROLLS

400g/14oz/3½ cups unbleached white
bread flour
7.5ml/1½ tsp salt
5ml/1 tsp caster (superfine) sugar
15g/½ oz fresh yeast
120ml/4fl oz/½ cup lukewarm milk
175ml/6fl oz/¾ cup lukewarm water

MAKES 10 ROLLS

A French and Belgian speciality, these attractive rolls are distinguished by the split down the centre. They have a crusty finish while remaining soft and light inside – they taste lovely, too.

1 Grease two baking sheets. Sift the flour and salt into a large bowl. Stir in the sugar and make a well in the centre.

2 Cream the yeast with the milk until dissolved, then pour into the centre of the flour mixture. Sprinkle over a little of the flour from around the edge. Leave at room temperature for 15–20 minutes, or until the mixture starts to bubble.

3 Add the water and gradually mix in the flour to form a fairly moist, soft dough. Turn out on to a lightly floured surface and knead for 8–10 minutes until smooth and elastic. Place in a lightly oiled bowl, cover with lightly oiled clear film (plastic wrap) and leave to rise, at room temperature, for about 1½ hours, or until doubled in bulk.

4 Turn out on to a lightly floured surface and knock back (punch down). Re-cover and leave to rest for 5 minutes. Divide into 10 pieces. Shape into balls by rolling the dough under a cupped hand, then roll until oval. Lightly flour the tops. Space well apart on the baking sheets, cover with lightly oiled clear film and leave at room temperature, for about 30 minutes, or until almost doubled in size.

5 Lightly oil the side of your hand and press the centre of each roll to make a deep split. Re-cover and leave to rest for 15 minutes. Meanwhile, place a roasting pan in the bottom of the oven and preheat the oven to 230°C/450°F/Gas 8. Pour 250ml/8fl oz/1 cup water into the tin and bake the rolls for 15 minutes, or until golden. Cool on a wire rack.

Per pain au lait Energy 169kcal/713kJ; Protein 4.3g; Carbohydrate 30.2g, of which sugars 1.6g; Fat 4.3g, of which saturates 2.5g; Cholesterol 10mg; Calcium 79mg; Fibre 1.2g; Sodium 36mg.
Per dimpled roll Energy 144kcal/610kJ; Protein 4.2g; Carbohydrate 32.1g, of which sugars 1.6g; Fat 0.7g, of which saturates 0.2g; Cholesterol 1mg; Calcium 71mg; Fibre 1.2g; Sodium 303mg.

KUGELHOPF

150g/5oz/⅔ cup unsalted (sweet) butter, softened
12 walnut halves
675g/1½lb/6 cups unbleached white bread flour
7.5ml/1½ tsp salt
20g/¾oz fresh yeast
300ml/10fl oz/1¼ cups milk
115g/4oz smoked bacon, diced
1 onion, finely chopped
15ml/1 tbsp vegetable oil
5 eggs, beaten
freshly ground black pepper

MAKES 1 LOAF

This inviting, fluted ring-shaped bread originates from Alsace, although Germany, Hungary and Austria all have their own variations of this popular recipe. Kugelhopf can be sweet or savoury; this version is richly flavoured with nuts, onion and bacon.

VARIATION
To make a sweet kugelhopf replace the walnuts with whole almonds and the bacon and onion with 115g/4oz/1 cup raisins and 50g/2oz/⅓ cup mixed chopped (candied) peel. Add 50g/2oz/¼ cup caster (superfine) sugar in step 2 and omit the black pepper.

1 Use 25g/1oz/2 tbsp of the butter to grease a 23cm/9in kugelhopf mould. Place eight walnut halves around the base and chop the remainder.

2 Sift the flour and salt together into a large bowl and season with pepper. Make a well in the centre. Cream the yeast with 45ml/3 tbsp of the milk. Pour into the centre of the flour with the remaining milk. Mix in a little flour to make a thick batter. Sprinkle a little of the remaining flour over the top of the batter, cover with clear film (plastic wrap) and leave in a warm place for 20–30 minutes until the yeast mixture bubbles.

3 Meanwhile, fry the bacon and onion in the oil until the onion is pale golden.

4 Add the eggs to the flour mixture and gradually beat in the flour, using your hand. Gradually beat in the remaining softened butter to form a soft dough. Cover with lightly oiled clear film and leave to rise, in a warm place, for 45–60 minutes, or until almost doubled in bulk. Preheat the oven to 200°C/400°F/Gas 6.

5 Knock back (punch down) the dough and gently knead in the bacon, onion and nuts. Place in the mould, cover with lightly oiled clear film and leave to rise, in a warm place, for about 1 hour, or until it has risen to the top of the mould.

6 Bake for 40–45 minutes, or until the loaf has browned and sounds hollow when tapped on the base. Cool in the mould for 5 minutes, then on a wire rack.

Per loaf Energy 3828kcal/16069kJ; Protein 84.1g; Carbohydrate 501.5g, of which sugars 174.8g; Fat 175.7g, of which saturates 70.1g; Cholesterol 816mg; Calcium 1047mg; Fibre 22.9g; Sodium 1000mg.

BRIOCHE

Rich and buttery yet light and airy, this wonderful loaf captures the essence of the classic French bread.

1 Sift the flour and salt together into a large bowl and make a well in the centre. Put the yeast in a measuring jug (cup) and stir in the milk.

2 Add the yeast mixture to the centre of the flour with the eggs and mix together to form a soft dough.

3 Using your hand, beat the dough for 4–5 minutes until smooth and elastic. Cream the butter and sugar together. Gradually add the butter mixture to the dough in small amounts, making sure it is incorporated before adding more. Beat until smooth, shiny and elastic.

350g/12oz/3 cups unbleached white bread flour
2.5ml/1/2 tsp salt
15g/1/2 oz fresh yeast
60ml/4 tbsp lukewarm milk
3 eggs, lightly beaten
175g/6oz/3/4 cup butter, softened
25g/1oz/2 tbsp caster (superfine) sugar

For the Glaze
1 egg yolk
15ml/1 tbsp milk

Makes 1 Loaf

4 Cover the bowl with lightly oiled clear film (plastic wrap) and leave the dough to rise, in a warm place, for 1–2 hours or until doubled in bulk.

5 Lightly knock back (punch down) the dough, then re-cover and place in the refrigerator for 8–10 hours or overnight.

6 Lightly grease a 1.6 litre/2³/4 pint/ scant 7 cup brioche mould. Turn the dough out on to a lightly floured surface. Cut off almost a quarter and set aside. Shape the rest into a ball and place in the prepared mould. Shape the reserved dough into an elongated egg shape. Using two or three fingers, make a hole in the centre of the large ball of dough. Gently press the narrow end of the egg-shaped dough into the hole.

7 Mix together the egg yolk and milk for the glaze, and brush a little over the brioche. Cover with lightly oiled clear film and leave to rise, in a warm place, for 1¹/2–2 hours, or until the dough nearly reaches the top of the mould.

8 Meanwhile, preheat the oven to 230°C/450°F/Gas 8. Brush the brioche with the remaining glaze and bake for 10 minutes.

9 Reduce the oven temperature to 190°C/375°F/Gas 5 and bake for a further 20–25 minutes, or until golden. Turn out on to a wire rack to cool.

Per loaf Energy 2830kcal/11835kJ; Protein 54.6g; Carbohydrate 301.1g, of which sugars 34.4g; Fat 165.2g, of which saturates 100.5g; Cholesterol 977mg; Calcium 687mg; Fibre 10.9g; Sodium 2550mg.

MEDITERRANEAN BREADS

The warm, rich flavours of the Mediterranean find their way into the breads. Olive oil, sun-dried tomatoes, olives, garlic and fresh herbs all feature in breads that are so delicious that they are now widely enjoyed all over the world. Ciabatta, panini all'olio rolls, focaccia and schiacciata are just a few examples. Spanish, Moroccan and Portuguese breads include local grains like corn and barley, together with seeds such as sesame, sunflower and pumpkin giving the breads an interesting taste and texture. Elaborate speciality breads are baked for religious festivals, the Christmas breads – christopsomo and Twelfth Night bread – being some of the most spectacular.

PUGLIESE

This classic Italian open-textured, soft-crumbed bread is moistened and flavoured with fruity olive oil. Its floured top gives it a true country feel.

FOR THE BIGA STARTER
175g/6oz/1¹⁄2 cups unbleached white bread flour
7g/¹⁄4 oz fresh yeast
90ml/6 tbsp lukewarm water

FOR THE DOUGH
225g/8oz/2 cups unbleached white bread flour, plus extra for dusting
225g/8oz/2 cups unbleached wholemeal (whole-wheat) bread flour
5ml/1 tsp caster (superfine) sugar
10ml/2 tsp salt
15g/¹⁄2 oz fresh yeast
275ml/9fl oz/generous 1 cup lukewarm water
75ml/5 tbsp extra virgin olive oil

MAKES 1 LARGE LOAF

VARIATION
Incorporate 150g/5oz/1 cup chopped black olives into the dough at the end of step 5 for extra olive flavour.

1 Sift the flour for the *biga* starter into a large bowl. Make a well in the centre. In a small bowl, cream the yeast with the water. Pour the liquid into the centre of the flour and gradually mix in the surrounding flour to form a firm dough.

2 Turn the dough out on to a lightly floured surface and knead for 5 minutes until smooth and elastic. Return to the bowl, cover with lightly oiled clear film (plastic wrap) and leave to rise, in a warm place, for 8–10 hours, or until the dough has risen well and is starting to collapse.

3 Lightly flour a baking sheet. Mix the flours, sugar and salt for the dough in a large bowl. Cream the yeast and the water in another large bowl, then stir in the *biga* and mix together.

4 Stir in the flour mixture a little at a time, then add the olive oil in the same way, and mix to a soft dough. Turn out on to a lightly floured surface and knead the dough for 8–10 minutes until smooth and elastic.

5 Place in a lightly oiled bowl, cover with lightly oiled clear film and leave to rise, in a warm place, for 1–1¹⁄2 hours, or until doubled in bulk.

6 Turn out on to a lightly floured surface and knock back (punch down). Gently pull out the edges and fold under to make a round. Transfer to the prepared baking sheet, cover with lightly oiled clear film and leave to rise, in a warm place, for 1–1¹⁄2 hours, or until almost doubled in size.

7 Meanwhile, preheat the oven to 230°C/ 450°F/Gas 8. Lightly dust the loaf with flour and bake for 15 minutes. Reduce the oven temperature to 200°C/400°F/ Gas 6 and bake for a further 20 minutes, or until the loaf sounds hollow when tapped on the base. Transfer to a wire rack to cool.

Per loaf Energy 2502kcal/10567kJ; Protein 72g; Carbohydrate 430.4g, of which sugars 11.8g; Fat 66.7g, of which saturates 9.5g; Cholesterol 0mg; Calcium 468mg; Fibre 43g; Sodium 3949mg.

CIABATTA

This irregular-shaped Italian bread is made with a very wet dough flavoured with olive oil; cooking produces a bread with holes and a chewy crust.

1 Cream the yeast for the *biga* starter with a little of the water. Sift the flour into a large bowl. Gradually mix in the yeast mixture and sufficient of the remaining water to form a firm dough.

2 Turn out the *biga* starter dough on to a lightly floured surface and knead for about 5 minutes until smooth and elastic. Return the dough to the bowl, cover with lightly oiled clear film (plastic wrap) and leave in a warm place for 12–15 hours, or until the dough has risen and is starting to collapse.

3 Sprinkle three baking sheets with flour. Mix the yeast for the dough with a little of the water until creamy, then mix in the remainder. Add the yeast mixture to the *biga* and gradually mix together.

4 Mix in the milk, beating thoroughly with a wooden spoon. Using your hand, gradually beat in the flour, lifting the dough as you mix. Mixing the dough will take 15 minutes or more and form a very wet mix, impossible to knead on a work surface.

5 Beat in the salt and olive oil. Cover with lightly oiled clear film and leave to rise, in a warm place, for 1½–2 hours, or until doubled in bulk.

6 With a spoon, carefully tip one-third of the dough at a time on to the baking sheets without knocking back (punching down) the dough in the process.

7 Using floured hands, shape into rough oblong loaf shapes, about 2.5cm/1in thick. Flatten slightly with splayed fingers. Sprinkle with flour and leave to rise in a warm place for 30 minutes.

8 Meanwhile, preheat the oven to 220°C/425°F/Gas 7. Bake for 25–30 minutes, or until golden brown and sounding hollow when tapped on the base. Transfer to a wire rack to cool.

For the Biga Starter
7g/¼ oz fresh yeast
175–200ml/6–7fl oz/¾–scant 1 cup lukewarm water
350g/12oz/3 cups unbleached plain (all-purpose) flour, plus extra for dusting

For the Dough
15g/½ oz fresh yeast
400ml/14fl oz/1⅔ cups lukewarm water
60ml/4 tbsp lukewarm milk
500g/1¼ lb/5 cups unbleached white bread flour
10ml/2 tsp salt
45ml/3 tbsp extra virgin olive oil

MAKES 3 LOAVES

VARIATION
To make tomato-flavoured ciabatta, add 115g/4oz/1 cup chopped, drained sun-dried tomatoes in olive oil. Add with the olive oil in step 5.

Per loaf Energy 985kcal/4176kJ; Protein 25g; Carbohydrate 202.8g, of which sugars 4.8g; Fat 13.8g, of which saturates 2.2g; Cholesterol 1mg; Calcium 386mg; Fibre 8.1g; Sodium 1217mg.

FOCACCIA

*20g/³⁄₄ oz fresh yeast
325–350ml/11–12fl oz/1¹⁄₃–1¹⁄₂ cups
lukewarm water
45ml/3 tbsp extra virgin olive oil
500g/1¹⁄₄ lb/5 cups unbleached white
bread flour
10ml/2 tsp salt
15ml/1 tbsp chopped fresh sage*

*For the Topping
60ml/4 tbsp extra virgin olive oil
4 garlic cloves, chopped
12 fresh sage leaves*

Makes 2 Round Loaves

This simple dimple-topped Italian flat bread is punctuated with olive oil and the aromatic flavours of sage and garlic to produce a truly succulent loaf.

VARIATION
Flavour the bread with other herbs, such as oregano, basil or rosemary and top with chopped black olives.

1 Lightly oil 2 × 25cm/10in shallow round cake tins (pans) or pizza pans. Cream the yeast with 60ml/4 tbsp of the water, then stir in the remaining water. Stir in the oil.

2 Sift the flour and salt together into a large bowl and make a well in the centre. Pour the yeast mixture into the well in the centre of the flour and mix to a soft dough.

3 Turn out the dough on to a lightly floured surface and knead for 8–10 minutes until smooth and elastic. Place in a lightly oiled bowl, cover with lightly oiled clear film (plastic wrap) or a large, lightly oiled plastic bag, and leave to rise, in a warm place, for about 1–1¹⁄₂ hours, or until doubled in bulk.

4 Knock back (punch down) and turn out on to a lightly floured surface. Gently knead in the chopped sage. Divide the dough into two equal pieces. Shape each into a ball, roll out into 25cm/10in circles and place in the prepared tins.

5 Cover with lightly oiled clear film and leave to rise in a warm place for about 30 minutes. Uncover, and using your fingertips, poke the dough to make deep dimples over the entire surface. Replace the clear film cover and leave to rise until doubled in bulk.

6 Meanwhile, preheat the oven to 200°C/ 400°F/Gas 6. Drizzle over the olive oil for the topping and sprinkle each focaccia evenly with chopped garlic. Dot the sage leaves over the surface. Bake for 25–30 minutes, or until both loaves are golden. Immediately remove the focaccia from the tins and transfer them to a wire rack to cool slightly. These loaves are best served warm.

Per loaf Energy 1661kcal/7020kJ; Protein 37.6g; Carbohydrate 310.8g, of which sugars 6g; Fat 38.2g, of which saturates 5.5g; Cholesterol 0mg; Calcium 561mg; Fibre 12.4g; Sodium 3942mg.

SESAME-STUDDED GRISSINI

*225g/8oz/2 cups unbleached white
bread flour
7.5ml/1½ tsp salt
15g/½ oz fresh yeast
135ml/4½ fl oz/scant ⅔ cup lukewarm
water
30ml/2 tbsp extra virgin olive oil,
plus extra for brushing
sesame seeds, for coating*

MAKES 20 GRISSINI

*These crisp, pencil-like breadsticks are easy to make and far more delicious
than the commercially manufactured grissini. Once you start to nibble one, it
will be difficult to stop.*

1 Lightly oil two baking sheets. Sift the flour and salt together into a large bowl and make a well in the centre.

2 In a jug (pitcher), cream the yeast with the water. Pour into the centre of the flour, add the olive oil and mix to a soft dough. Turn out on to a lightly floured surface and knead for 8–10 minutes until smooth and elastic.

3 Roll the dough into a rectangle about 15 × 20cm/6 × 8in. Brush with olive oil, cover with lightly oiled clear film (plastic wrap) and leave in a warm place, for about 1 hour, or until doubled in bulk.

4 Preheat the oven to 200°C/400°F/ Gas 6. Spread out the sesame seeds. Cut the dough in two 7.5 x 10cm/3 x 4in rectangles. Cut each piece into ten 7.5cm/3in strips. Stretch each strip gently until it is about 30cm/12in long.

5 Roll each grissini, as it is made, in the sesame seeds. Place the grissini on the prepared baking sheets, spaced well apart. Lightly brush with olive oil. Leave to rise, in a warm place, for 10 minutes, then bake for 15–20 minutes. Transfer to a wire rack to cool.

COOK'S TIP
When baking the grissini turn them over and change the position of the baking sheets halfway through the cooking time, so they brown evenly.

PIADINE

*175g/6oz/1½ cups unbleached
white flour
5ml/1 tsp salt
15ml/1 tbsp olive oil
105ml/7 tbsp lukewarm water*

MAKES 4 PIADINE

*These soft unleavened Italian breads, cooked directly on the hob, were
originally cooked on a hot stone over an open fire. They are best eaten while
still warm. Try them as an accompaniment to soups and dips.*

1 Sift the flour and salt together into a large bowl; make a well in the centre.

2 Add the oil and water to the centre of the flour and gradually mix in to form a dough. Knead on a lightly floured surface for 4–5 minutes until smooth and elastic. Place in a lightly oiled bowl, cover with oiled clear film (plastic wrap) and leave to rest for 20 minutes.

3 Heat a griddle over a medium heat. Divide the dough into four equal pieces and roll each into an 18cm/7in round. Cover until ready to cook.

4 Lightly oil the hot griddle, add one or two piadine and cook for about 2 minutes, or until they are starting to brown. Turn the piadine over and cook for a further 1–1½ minutes. Serve warm.

COOK'S TIPS
• If you don't have a griddle, a large heavy frying pan will work just as well. Keep the cooked piadine warm while cooking successive batches.
• Although not traditional in Italy, these flat breads can also be flavoured with herbs. Add 15ml/1 tbsp of dried oregano. They also taste delicious made with garlic- or chilli-flavoured olive oil.

Per grissini Energy 53kcal/223kJ; Protein 1.2g; Carbohydrate 8.8g, of which sugars 0.2g; Fat 1.7g, of which saturates 0.2g; Cholesterol 0mg; Calcium 21mg; Fibre 0.4g; Sodium 148mg.
Per piadine Energy 174kcal/736kJ; Protein 4.1g; Carbohydrate 34g, of which sugars 0.7g; Fat 3.3g, of which saturates 0.5g; Cholesterol 0mg; Calcium 62mg; Fibre 1.4g; Sodium 493mg.

PANETTONE

400g/14oz/3½ cups unbleached white
bread flour
2.5ml/½ tsp salt
15g/½ oz fresh yeast
120ml/4fl oz/½ cup lukewarm milk
2 eggs plus 2 egg yolks
75g/3oz/6 tbsp caster (superfine) sugar
150g/5oz/⅔ cup butter, softened
115g/4oz/⅔ cup mixed chopped
(candied) peel
75g/3oz/½ cup raisins
melted butter, for brushing

MAKES 1 LOAF

COOK'S TIP
Once the dough has been enriched
with butter, do not prove in too warm
a place or the loaf will become greasy.

This classic Italian bread can be found throughout Italy around Christmas.
It is a surprisingly light bread even though it is rich with butter
and dried fruit.

1 Using a double layer of baking parchment, line and butter a 15cm/6in deep cake tin (pan) or soufflé dish. Finish the paper 7.5cm/3in above the top of the tin.

2 Sift the flour and salt together into a large bowl. Make a well in the centre. Cream the yeast with 60ml/4 tbsp of the milk, then mix in the remainder.

3 Pour the yeast mixture into the centre of the flour, add the whole eggs and mix in sufficient flour to make a thick batter. Sprinkle a little of the remaining flour over the top and leave to "sponge", in a warm place, for 30 minutes.

4 Add the egg yolks and sugar and mix to a soft dough. Work in the softened butter, then turn out on to a lightly floured surface and knead for 5 minutes until smooth and elastic. Place in a lightly oiled bowl, cover with lightly oiled clear film (plastic wrap) and leave to rise, in a slightly warm place, for 1½–2 hours, or until doubled in bulk.

5 Knock back (punch down) the dough and turn out on to a lightly floured surface. Gently knead in the peel and raisins. Shape into a ball and place in the prepared tin. Cover with lightly oiled clear film and leave to rise, in a slightly warm place, for about 1 hour, or until doubled.

6 Meanwhile, preheat the oven to 190°C/375°F/Gas 5. Brush the surface with melted butter and cut a cross in the top using a sharp knife. Bake for 20 minutes, then reduce the oven temperature to 180°C/350°F/Gas 4. Brush the top with butter again and bake for a further 25–30 minutes, or until golden. Cool in the tin for 5–10 minutes, then turn out on to a wire rack to cool.

Per loaf Energy 2453kcal/10412kJ; Protein 62.2g; Carbohydrate 515.1g, of which sugars 210.3g; Fat 30.7g, of which saturates 8.2g; Cholesterol 791mg; Calcium 1032mg; Fibre 19.4g; Sodium 1590mg.

PANE AL CIOCCOLATO

This slightly sweet chocolate bread from Italy is often served with creamy mascarpone cheese as a dessert or snack. The dark chocolate pieces add texture to this light loaf.

350g/12oz/3 cups unbleached white bread flour
25ml/1½ tbsp cocoa powder (unsweetened)
2.5ml/½ tsp salt
25g/1oz/2 tbsp caster (superfine) sugar
15g/½ oz fresh yeast
250ml/8fl oz/1 cup lukewarm water
25g/1oz/2 tbsp butter, softened
75g/3oz plain continental chocolate, coarsely chopped
melted butter, for brushing

MAKES 1 LOAF

1 Lightly grease a 15cm/6in round deep cake tin (pan). Sift the flour, cocoa powder and salt together into a large bowl. Stir in the sugar. Make a well in the centre.

2 Cream the yeast with 60ml/4 tbsp of the water, then stir in the rest. Add to the centre of the flour mixture and gradually mix to a dough.

3 Knead in the softened butter, then knead on a floured surface until smooth and elastic. Place in a lightly oiled bowl, cover with lightly oiled clear film (plastic wrap) and leave in a warm place, for about 1 hour, or until doubled in bulk.

4 Turn out on to a lightly floured surface and knock back (punch down). Gently knead in the chocolate, then cover with oiled clear film; rest for 5 minutes.

5 Shape the dough into a round and place in the tin. Cover with lightly oiled clear film and leave to rise, in a warm place, for 45 minutes, or until doubled; the dough should reach the top of the tin.

6 Preheat the oven to 220°C/425°F/Gas 7. Bake for 10 minutes, then reduce the oven temperature to 190°C/375°F/Gas 5 and bake for a further 25–30 minutes. Brush the top with melted butter and leave to cool on a wire rack.

VARIATION
You can also shape this bread into one large, or two small rounds and bake on a lightly greased baking sheet. Reduce the baking time by about 10 minutes.

Per loaf Energy 1939kcal/8188kJ; Protein 41.5g; Carbohydrate 348.7g, of which sugars 78.5g; Fat 51.5g, of which saturates 29.5g; Cholesterol 58mg; Calcium 565mg; Fibre 15.8g; Sodium 406mg.

SCHIACCIATA

This Tuscan version of Italian pizza-style flat bread can be rolled to varying thicknesses to give either a crisp or soft, bread-like finish.

350g/12oz/3 cups unbleached white bread flour
2.5ml/½ tsp salt
15g/½ oz fresh yeast
200ml/7fl oz/scant 1 cup lukewarm water
60ml/4 tbsp extra virgin olive oil

FOR THE TOPPING
30ml/2 tbsp extra virgin olive oil, for brushing
30ml/2 tbsp fresh rosemary leaves
coarse sea salt, for sprinkling

MAKES 1 LARGE LOAF

1 Lightly oil a baking sheet. Sift the flour and salt into a large bowl and make a well in the centre. Cream the yeast with half the water. Add to the centre of the flour with the remaining water and olive oil and mix to a soft dough. Turn out the dough on to a lightly floured surface and knead for 10 minutes until smooth and elastic.

2 Place in a lightly oiled bowl, cover with lightly oiled clear film (plastic wrap) and leave to rise, in a warm place, for about 1 hour, or until doubled in bulk.

3 Knock back (punch down) the dough, turn out on to a lightly floured surface and knead gently. Roll to a 30 × 20cm/ 12 × 8in rectangle and place on the prepared baking sheet. Brush with some of the olive oil for the topping and cover with lightly oiled clear film.

4 Leave to rise, in a warm place, for about 20 minutes, then brush with the remaining oil, prick all over with a fork and sprinkle with rosemary and sea salt. Leave to rise again in a warm place for 15 minutes.

5 Meanwhile, preheat the oven to 200°C/ 400°F/Gas 6. Bake for 30 minutes, or until light golden. Transfer to a wire rack to cool slightly. Serve warm.

Per loaf Energy 1436kcal/6068kJ; Protein 34.8g; Carbohydrate 266g, of which sugars 5.1g; Fat 33.1g, of which saturates 4.5g; Cholesterol 0mg; Calcium 574mg; Fibre 10.5g; Sodium 18mg.

PORTUGUESE CORN BREAD

While the Spanish make a corn bread with barley flour, the Portuguese use white bread flour and corn meal. This tempting version has a hard crust with a moist, mouthwatering crumb. It slices beautifully and tastes wonderful served simply with butter or olive oil, or with cheese.

20g/¾ oz fresh yeast
250ml/8fl oz/1 cup lukewarm water
225g/8oz/2 cups corn meal
450g/1lb/4 cups unbleached white bread flour
150ml/¼ pint/⅔ cup lukewarm milk
30ml/2 tbsp olive oil
7.5ml/1½ tsp salt
polenta, for dusting

MAKES 1 LARGE LOAF

VARIATION
Replace 50 per cent of the corn meal with polenta for a rougher textured, slightly crunchier loaf.

1 Dust a baking sheet with a little corn meal. Put the yeast in a large bowl and gradually mix in the lukewarm water until smooth. Stir in half the corn meal and 50g/2oz/½ cup of the flour and mix to a batter, with a wooden spoon.

6 Turn out the dough on to a lightly floured surface and knock back (punch down). Shape into a round ball, flatten slightly and place on the prepared baking sheet. Dust with polenta, cover with a large upturned bowl and leave to rise, in a warm place, for about 1 hour, or until doubled in size. Meanwhile, preheat the oven to 230°C/450°F/Gas 8.

7 Bake for 10 minutes, spraying the inside of the oven with water two or three times. Reduce the temperature to 190°C/375°F/Gas 5 and bake for a further 20–25 minutes, or until golden and hollow sounding when tapped on the base. Transfer to a wire rack to cool.

2 Cover the bowl with lightly oiled clear film (plastic wrap) and leave the batter undisturbed in a warm place for about 30 minutes, or until bubbles start to appear on the surface. Remove the film.

3 Stir the milk into the batter, then stir in the olive oil. Gradually mix in the remaining corn meal, flour and salt to form a pliable dough.

4 Turn out the dough on to a lightly floured surface and knead for about 10 minutes until smooth and elastic.

5 Place in a lightly oiled bowl, cover with lightly oiled clear film and leave to rise, in a warm place, for 1½–2 hours, or until doubled in bulk.

Per loaf Energy 3008kcal/12539kJ; Protein 52.7g; Carbohydrate 303.3g, of which sugars 87.7g; Fat 179.8g, of which saturates 46.1g; Cholesterol 561mg; Calcium 696mg; Fibre 7.4g; Sodium 1672mg.

PAN GALLEGO

Here, a typical round bread with a twisted top from Galicia. The olive oil gives a soft crumb and the millet, pumpkin and sunflower seeds sprinkled through the loaf provide an interesting mix of textures.

350g/12oz/3 cups unbleached white bread flour
115g/4oz/1 cup wholemeal (whole-wheat) bread flour
10ml/2 tsp salt
20g/¾ oz fresh yeast
275ml/9fl oz/generous 1 cup lukewarm water
30ml/2 tbsp olive oil
30ml/2 tbsp pumpkin seeds
30ml/2 tbsp sunflower seeds
15ml/1 tbsp millet
corn meal, for dusting

MAKES 1 LARGE LOAF

COOK'S TIP
If you like, replace fresh yeast with a 7g/¼ oz sachet of easy bake (rapid-rise) dried yeast. Stir into the flours in step 1. Continue as in the recipe.

1 Sprinkle a baking sheet with corn meal. Mix the flours and salt together in a large bowl.

2 In a bowl, mix the yeast with the water. Add to the centre of the flours with the olive oil and mix to a firm dough. Turn out on to a lightly floured surface and knead for about 10 minutes until smooth and elastic. Place in a lightly oiled bowl, then cover with lightly oiled clear film (plastic wrap) and leave to rise, in a warm place, for about 1½–2 hours, or until doubled in bulk.

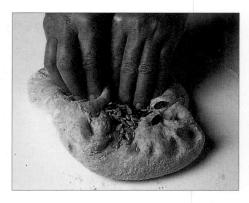

3 Knock back (punch down) the dough and turn out on to a lightly floured surface. Gently knead in the pumpkin seeds, sunflower seeds and millet. Re-cover and leave to rest for 5 minutes.

4 Shape into a round ball; twist the centre to make a cap. Transfer to the prepared baking sheet and dust with corn meal. Cover with a large upturned bowl and leave to rise, in a warm place, for 45 minutes, or until doubled in bulk.

5 Meanwhile, place an empty roasting pan in the bottom of the oven. Preheat the oven to 220°C/425°F/Gas 7. Pour about 300ml/½ pint/1¼ cups cold water into the roasting pan. Lift the bowl off the risen loaf and immediately place the baking sheet in the oven, above the roasting pan. Bake the bread for 10 minutes.

6 Remove the tin of water and bake the bread for a further 25–30 minutes, or until well browned and sounding hollow when tapped on the base. Transfer to a wire rack to cool.

Per loaf Energy 1668kcal/7038kJ; Protein 47g; Carbohydrate 276.1g, of which sugars 6.9g; Fat 49.1g, of which saturates 6g; Cholesterol 0mg; Calcium 443mg; Fibre 20.8g; Sodium 12mg.

PAN DE CEBADA

This Spanish country bread has a close, heavy texture and is quite satisfying.
It is richly flavoured, incorporating barley and maize flours.

FOR THE SOURDOUGH STARTER
175g/6oz/1½ cups corn meal
560ml/scant 1 pint/scant 2½ cups
water
225g/8oz/2 cups wholemeal
(whole-wheat) bread flour
75g/3oz/¾ cup barley flour

FOR THE DOUGH
20g/¾ oz fresh yeast
45ml/3 tbsp lukewarm water
225g/8oz/2 cups wholemeal
bread flour
15ml/1 tbsp salt
corn meal, for dusting

MAKES 1 LARGE LOAF

1 In a pan, mix the corn meal for the sourdough starter with half the water, then blend in the remainder. Cook over a gentle heat, stirring continuously, until thickened. Transfer to a large bowl and set aside to cool.

2 Mix in the wholemeal flour and barley flour. Turn out on to a lightly floured surface and knead for 5 minutes. Return to the bowl, cover with lightly oiled clear film (plastic wrap) and leave the starter in a warm place for 36 hours.

5 Knock back (punch down) the dough and turn out on to a lightly floured surface. Shape into a plump round. Sprinkle with a little corn meal.

6 Place the shaped bread on the prepared baking sheet. Cover with a large upturned bowl. Leave to rise, in a warm place, for about 1 hour, or until nearly doubled in bulk. Place an empty roasting pan in the bottom of the oven. Preheat the oven to 220°C/425°F/Gas 7.

7 Pour 300ml/½ pint/1¼ cups cold water into the roasting pan. Lift the bowl off the risen loaf and immediately place the baking sheet in the oven. Bake the bread for 10 minutes. Remove the pan of water, reduce the oven temperature to 190°C/375°F/Gas 5 and bake for about 20 minutes. Cool on a wire rack.

3 Dust a baking sheet with corn meal. In a small bowl, cream the yeast with the water for the dough. Mix the yeast mixture into the starter with the wholemeal flour and salt and work to a dough. Turn out on to a lightly floured surface and knead for 4–5 minutes until smooth and elastic.

4 Transfer the dough to a lightly oiled bowl, cover with lightly oiled clear film or an oiled plastic bag and leave, in a warm place, for 1½–2 hours to rise, or until nearly doubled in bulk.

Per loaf Energy 2265kcal/9588kJ; Protein 81.5g; Carbohydrate 463.5g, of which sugars 10.8g; Fat 17.2g, of which saturates 1.4g; Cholesterol 0mg; Calcium 214mg; Fibre 55.4g; Sodium 16mg.

TWELFTH NIGHT BREAD

*450g/1lb/4 cups unbleached white
bread flour
2.5ml/½ tsp salt
25g/1oz fresh yeast
140ml/scant ¼ pint/scant ⅔ cup
mixed lukewarm milk and water
75g/3oz/6 tbsp butter
75g/3oz/6 tbsp caster
(superfine) sugar
10ml/2 tsp finely grated
lemon rind
10ml/2 tsp finely grated
orange rind
2 eggs
15ml/1 tbsp brandy
15ml/1 tbsp orange flower water
silver coin or dried bean
(optional)
1 egg white, lightly beaten,
for glazing*

*FOR THE DECORATION
a mixture of candied and glacé
fruit slices
flaked (sliced) almonds*

MAKES 1 LARGE LOAF

*January 6th, Epiphany or the Day of the Three Kings, is celebrated in
Spain as a time to exchange Christmas presents. Historically this date was
when the Three Wise Men arrived bearing gifts. An ornamental bread ring is
specially baked for the occasion. The traditional version contains a silver
coin, china figure or dried bean hidden inside – the lucky recipient is
declared King of the festival!*

2 In a bowl, mix the yeast with the milk and water until the yeast has dissolved. Pour the yeast mixture into the centre of the flour and stir in enough of the flour from around the sides of the bowl to make a thick batter.

3 Sprinkle a little of the remaining flour over the top of the batter and leave to "sponge", in a warm place, for about 15 minutes or until frothy.

4 Using an electric whisk or a wooden spoon, beat the butter and sugar together in a bowl until soft and creamy, then set aside.

5 Add the citrus rinds, eggs, brandy and orange flower water to the flour mixture and use a wooden spoon to mix to a sticky dough.

8 Using a rolling pin, roll out the dough into a long strip measuring about 66 × 13cm/26 × 5in.

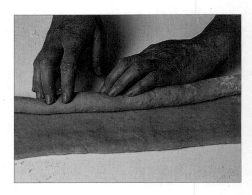

9 Roll up the dough from one long side like a Swiss roll to make a long sausage shape. Place seam side down on the prepared baking sheet and seal the ends together. Cover with lightly oiled clear film and leave to rise, in a warm place, for 1–1½ hours, or until doubled in size.

COOK'S TIP

If you like, this bread can be baked in a lightly greased 24cm/9½ in ring-shaped cake tin (pan) or savarin mould. Place the dough seam side down into the tin or mould and seal the ends together.

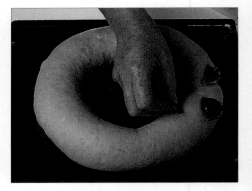

6 Using one hand, beat the mixture until it forms a fairly smooth dough. Gradually beat in the reserved butter mixture and beat for a few minutes until the dough is smooth and elastic. Cover with lightly oiled clear film (plastic wrap) and leave in a warm place, for about 1½ hours, or until doubled in bulk.

10 Meanwhile, preheat the oven to 180°C/350°F/Gas 4. Brush the dough ring with lightly beaten egg white and decorate with candied and glacé fruit slices, pushing them slightly into the dough. Sprinkle with almond flakes and bake for 30–35 minutes, or until risen and golden. Turn out on to a wire rack to cool.

1 Lightly grease a large baking sheet. Sift the flour and salt together into a large bowl. Make a well in the centre.

7 Knock back (punch down) the dough and turn out on to a lightly floured surface. Gently knead for 2–3 minutes, incorporating the coin or bean, if using.

Per loaf Energy 2784kcal/11739kJ; Protein 60.3g; Carbohydrate 464.4g, of which sugars 92.8g; Fat 85.2g, of which saturates 46.7g; Cholesterol 586mg; Calcium 802mg; Fibre 15.1g; Sodium 664mg.

MALLORCAN ENSAIMADAS

*225g/8oz/2 cups unbleached white
bread flour
2.5ml/½ tsp salt
50g/2oz/¼ cup caster (superfine) sugar
15g/½ oz fresh yeast
75ml/5 tbsp lukewarm milk
1 egg
30ml/2 tbsp sunflower oil
50g/2oz/¼ cup butter, melted
icing (confectioners') sugar, for dusting*

MAKES 16 ROLLS

These spiral- or snail-shaped rolls are a popular Spanish breakfast treat. Traditionally lard or saim *was used to brush over the strips of sweetened dough, but nowadays mainly butter is used to add a delicious richness.*

1 Lightly grease two baking sheets. Sift the flour and salt together into a large mixing bowl. Stir in the sugar and make a well in the centre.

2 Cream the yeast with the milk, pour into the centre of the flour mixture, then sprinkle a little of the flour mixture evenly over the top of the liquid. Leave in a warm place for about 15 minutes, or until frothy.

3 In a small bowl, beat the egg and sunflower oil together. Add to the flour mixture and mix to a smooth dough.

4 Turn out on to a lightly floured surface and knead for 8–10 minutes until smooth and elastic. Place in a lightly oiled bowl, cover with lightly oiled clear film (plastic wrap) and leave in a warm place, for 1 hour, or until doubled in bulk.

5 Turn out the dough on to a lightly floured surface. Knock back (punch down) and divide the dough into 16 equal pieces. Shape each piece into a thin rope about 38cm/15in long. Pour the melted butter on to a plate and dip the ropes into the butter to coat.

6 On the baking sheets, curl each rope into a loose spiral, spacing well apart. Tuck the ends under to seal. Cover with lightly oiled clear film and leave to rise, in a warm place, for about 45 minutes, or until doubled in size.

7 Meanwhile, preheat the oven to 190°C/375°F/Gas 5. Brush the rolls with water and dust with icing sugar. Bake for 10 minutes, or until light golden brown. Cool on a wire rack. Dust again with icing sugar and serve warm.

Per roll Energy 327kcal/1371kJ; Protein 8.7g; Carbohydrate 38.6g, of which sugars 4.3g; Fat 16.1g, of which saturates 9.3g; Cholesterol 117mg; Calcium 172mg; Fibre 1.4g; Sodium 162mg.

PITTA BREAD

These Turkish breads are a firm favourite in both the eastern Mediterranean and the Middle East, and have crossed to England and the USA. This versatile soft, flat bread forms a pocket as it cooks, which is perfect for filling with vegetables, salads or meats.

225g/8oz/2 cups unbleached white bread flour
5ml/1 tsp salt
15g/¹/₂ oz fresh yeast
140ml/scant ¹/₄ pint/scant ²/₃ cup lukewarm water
10ml/2 tsp extra virgin olive oil

MAKES 6 PITTA BREADS

VARIATIONS
To make wholemeal (whole-wheat) pitta breads, replace half the white bread flour with wholemeal bread flour. You can also make smaller round pitta breads about 10cm/4in in diameter to serve as snack breads.

5 Roll out each ball of dough in turn to an oval about 5mm/¹/₄in thick and 15cm/6in long. Place on a floured dishtowel and cover with lightly oiled clear film. Leave to rise at room temperature for about 20–30 minutes.

6 Meanwhile, preheat the oven to 230ºC/450ºF/Gas 8. Place three baking sheets in the oven to heat at the same time.

7 Place two pitta breads on each baking sheet and bake for 4–6 minutes, or until puffed up; they do not need to brown. If preferred, cook the pitta bread in batches. It is important that the oven has reached the recommended temperature before the pitta breads are baked. This ensures that they puff up.

8 Transfer the pittas to a wire rack to cool until warm, then cover with a dishtowel to keep them soft.

1 Sift the flour and salt together into a bowl. Mix the yeast with the water until dissolved, then stir in the olive oil and pour into a large bowl.

2 Gradually beat the flour into the yeast mixture, then knead the mixture to make a soft dough.

3 Turn out on to a lightly floured surface and knead for 5 minutes until smooth and elastic. Place in a large bowl, cover with lightly oiled clear film (plastic wrap) and leave to rise, in a warm place, for 1 hour, or until doubled in bulk.

4 Knock back (punch down) the dough. On a floured surface, divide into six equal pieces and shape into balls. Cover with oiled clear film; rest for 5 minutes.

Per pitta Energy 150kcal/638kJ; Protein 3.9g; Carbohydrate 32.4g, of which sugars 0.6g; Fat 1.5g, of which saturates 0.2g; Cholesterol 0mg; Calcium 59mg; Fibre 1.3g; Sodium 493mg.

Per loaf Energy 1551kcal/6450kJ; Protein 45.9g; Carbohydrate 262.1g, of which sugars 10.8g; Fat 58.9g, of which saturates 5.0g; Cholesterol 7mg; Calcium 765mg; Fibre 13.8g; Sodium 2040mg.

NORTH EUROPEAN AND SCANDINAVIAN BREADS

The northern Europeans and Scandinavians make many different loaves, from German sourdough bread with its distinctive flavour to the light-crumbed Swiss braid. Also from these northern climes come the famous Swedish crispbreads, Russian potato bread and blinis, lightly scented saffron buns and port-flavoured rye bread. Christmas breads are enriched with fruit, while Bulgaria has its own poppy-seeded bread for religious festivals.

Per loaf Energy 2065kcal/8793kJ; Protein 59.8g; Carbohydrate 459.1g, of which sugars 5.4g; Fat 11.7g, of which saturates 1.7g; Cholesterol 0mg; Calcium 372mg; Fibre 56.2g; Sodium 3942mg.

75g/3oz/¹/2 cup sultanas (golden raisins)
50g/2oz/¹/4 cup currants
45ml/3 tbsp rum
375g/13oz/3¹/4 cups unbleached white
bread flour
2.5ml/¹/2 tsp salt
50g/2oz/¹/4 cup caster (superfine)
sugar
1.5ml/¹/4 tsp ground cardamom
2.5ml/¹/2 tsp ground cinnamon
40g/1¹/2 oz fresh yeast
120ml/4fl oz/¹/2 cup lukewarm milk
50g/2oz/¹/4 cup butter, melted
1 egg, lightly beaten
50g/2oz/¹/3 cup mixed (candied) peel
50g/2oz/¹/3 cup blanched whole
almonds, chopped
melted butter, for brushing
icing (confectioners') sugar to dust

FOR THE ALMOND FILLING
115g/4oz/1 cup ground almonds
50g/2oz/¹/4 cup caster sugar
50g/2oz/¹/2 cup icing sugar
2.5ml/¹/2 tsp lemon juice
¹/2 egg, lightly beaten

MAKES 1 LARGE LOAF

COOK'S TIP
You can dust the cooled stollen with
icing sugar and cinnamon, or drizzle
over a thin glacé icing.

1 Lightly grease a baking sheet. Preheat
the oven to 180°C/350°F/Gas 4. Put the
sultanas and currants in a heatproof
bowl and warm for 3–4 minutes. Pour
over the rum and set aside.

2 Sift the flour and salt together into a
large bowl. Stir in the sugar and spices.

STOLLEN

*This German speciality bread, made for the Christmas season, is rich with
rum-soaked fruits and is wrapped around a moist almond filling. The folded
shape of the dough over the filling represents the baby Jesus wrapped in
swaddling clothes.*

3 Mix the yeast with the milk until
creamy. Pour into the flour and mix a
little of the flour from around the edge
into the milk mixture to make a thick
batter. Sprinkle some of the remaining
flour over the top of the batter, then
cover with clear film (plastic wrap) and
leave in a warm place for 30 minutes.

4 Add the melted butter and egg and
mix to a soft dough. Turn out the dough
on to a lightly floured surface and knead
for 8–10 minutes until smooth and
elastic. Place in a lightly oiled bowl,
cover with lightly oiled clear film and
leave to rise, in a warm place, for
2–3 hours, or until doubled in bulk.

5 Mix the ground almonds and sugars
together for the filling. Add the lemon
juice and sufficient egg to knead to a
smooth paste. Shape into a 20cm/8in
long sausage, cover and set aside.

6 Turn out the dough on to a lightly floured
surface and knock back (punch down).

7 Pat out the dough into a rectangle
about 2.5cm/1in thick and sprinkle over
the sultanas, currants, mixed peel and
almonds. Fold and knead the dough to
incorporate the fruit and nuts.

8 Roll out the dough into an oval about
30 × 23cm/12 × 9in. Roll the centre
slightly thinner than the edges. Place
the almond paste filling along the centre
and fold over the dough to enclose it,
making sure that the top of the dough
doesn't completely cover the base. The
top edge should be slightly in from
the bottom edge. Press down to seal.

9 Place the loaf on the prepared baking
sheet, cover with lightly oiled clear film
and leave to rise, in a warm place, for
45–60 minutes, or until doubled in size.

10 Meanwhile, preheat the oven to
200°C/400°F/Gas 6. Bake the loaf for
about 30 minutes, or until it sounds
hollow when tapped on the base. Brush
the top with melted butter and transfer
to a wire rack to cool. Dust with icing
sugar just before serving.

Per loaf Energy 3828kcal/16064kJ; Protein 55.8g; Carbohydrate 511.7g, of which sugars 256.5g; Fat 178.8g, of which saturates 95.2g; Cholesterol 393mg; Calcium 1064mg; Fibre 21.5g;
Sodium 1590mg.

BUCHTY

*Popular in both Poland and Germany as breakfast treats, these are also
excellent split and toasted, and served with cured meats.*

*450g/1lb/4 cups unbleached white
bread flour
5ml/1 tsp salt
50g/2oz/¼ cup caster (superfine) sugar
90g/3½oz/scant ½ cup butter
120ml/4fl oz/½ cup milk
20g/¾ oz fresh yeast
3 eggs, lightly beaten
40g/1½ oz/3 tbsp butter, melted
icing (confectioners') sugar, for dusting*

MAKES 16 ROLLS

COOK'S TIP
If you do not have a square tin use a
round one. Place two rolls in the
centre and the rest around the edge.

1 Grease a 20cm/8in square loose-
bottomed cake tin (pan). Sift the flour and
salt together into a large bowl and stir in
the sugar. Make a well in the centre.

2 Melt 50g/2oz/¼ cup of the butter in a
small pan, then remove from the heat
and stir in the milk. Leave to cool until
lukewarm. Stir the yeast into the milk
mixture until it has dissolved.

3 Pour into the centre of the flour and
stir in sufficient flour to form a thick
batter. Sprinkle with a little of the
surrounding flour, cover and leave in a
warm place for 30 minutes.

4 Gradually beat in the eggs and
remaining flour to form a soft, smooth
dough. This will take about 10 minutes.
Cover with oiled clear film (plastic
wrap) and leave in a warm place, for
about 1½ hours, or until doubled in bulk.

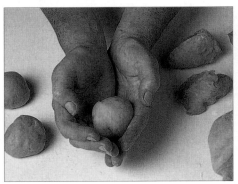

5 Turn out the dough on to a lightly floured
surface and knock back (punch down).
Divide into 16 equal pieces and shape
into rounds. Melt the remaining butter,
roll the rounds in it to coat, then place,
slightly apart, in the tin. Cover with lightly
oiled clear film and leave to rise, in a warm
place, for about 1 hour, or until doubled.

6 Meanwhile, preheat the oven to 190°C/
375°F/Gas 5. Spoon any remaining
melted butter evenly over the rolls and
bake for 25 minutes, or until golden
brown. Turn out on to a wire rack to
cool. If serving buchty as a breakfast
bread, dust the loaf with icing sugar
before separating it into rolls.

Per roll Energy 185kcal/779kJ; Protein 4.1g; Carbohydrate 25.5g, of which sugars 4.1g; Fat 8.2g, of which saturates 4.8g; Cholesterol 55mg; Calcium 57mg; Fibre 0.9g; Sodium 79mg.

POLISH RYE BREAD

This rye bread is made with half white flour which gives it a lighter, more open texture than a traditional rye loaf. Served thinly sliced, it is the perfect accompaniment for cold meats and fish.

225g/8oz/2 cups rye flour
225g/8oz/2 cups unbleached white bread flour
10ml/2 tsp caraway seeds
10ml/2 tsp salt
20g/¾ oz fresh yeast
140ml/scant ¼ pint/scant ⅔ cup lukewarm milk
5ml/1 tsp clear honey
140ml/scant ¼ pint/scant ⅔ cup lukewarm water
wholemeal (whole-wheat) flour, to dust

MAKES 1 LOAF

1 Lightly grease a baking sheet. Mix the flours, caraway seeds and salt in a large bowl and make a well in the centre.

2 In a bowl or measuring jug (cup), cream the yeast with the milk and honey. Pour into the centre of the flour, add the water and gradually incorporate the surrounding flour and caraway mixture until a dough forms.

3 Turn out the dough on to a lightly floured surface and knead for 8–10 minutes until smooth, elastic and firm. Place in a large, lightly oiled bowl, cover with lightly oiled clear film (plastic wrap) and leave in a warm place, for about 3 hours, or until doubled in bulk.

4 Turn out the dough on to a lightly floured surface and knock back (punch down). Shape into an oval loaf and place on the prepared baking sheet.

5 Dust with wholemeal flour, cover with lightly oiled clear film and leave to rise, in a warm place, for 1–1½ hours, or until doubled in size. Meanwhile, preheat the oven to 220°C/425°F/Gas 7.

6 Using a sharp knife, slash the loaf with two long cuts about 2.5cm/1in apart. Bake for 30–35 minutes, or until the loaf sounds hollow when tapped on the base. Transfer the loaf to a wire rack and set aside to cool.

Per loaf Energy 1667kcal/7088kJ; Protein 46.4g; Carbohydrate 360.2g, of which sugars 16.2g; Fat 14.6g, of which saturates 3.1g; Cholesterol 8mg; Calcium 567mg; Fibre 33.9g; Sodium 4000mg.

675g/1½ lb/6 cups unbleached white
bread flour
10ml/2 tsp salt
25g/1oz fresh yeast
120ml/4fl oz/½ cup lukewarm milk
5ml/1 tsp clear honey
2 eggs
150ml/¼ pint/⅔ cup natural
(plain) yogurt
50g/2oz/¼ cup butter, melted
beaten egg, for glazing
poppy seeds, for sprinkling

MAKES 1 LARGE LOAF

VARIATION
For a special finish, divide the dough
into three equal pieces, roll into long
thin strips and braid together, starting
with the centre of the strips. Once
plaited, shape into a circle and seal
the ends together. Make sure the hole
in the centre is quite large, otherwise
the hole will fill in as the bread rises.

KOLACH

*Often prepared for religious celebrations and family feasts, this Bulgarian
bread gets its name from its circular shape – kolo, which means circle. It has
a golden crust sprinkled with poppy seeds and a moist crumb, which makes
this loaf a very good keeper.*

1 Grease a large baking sheet. Sift the
flour and salt together into a large bowl
and make a well in the centre.

2 Cream the yeast with the milk and
honey. Add to the centre of the flour
with the eggs, yogurt and melted butter.
Gradually mix into the flour to form a
firm dough.

3 Turn out on to a lightly floured surface
and knead for 8–10 minutes until
smooth and elastic. Place in a lightly
oiled bowl, cover with lightly oiled clear
film (plastic wrap) or slip into an oiled
plastic bag. Leave in a warm place, for
1½ hours, or until doubled in bulk.

4 Knock back (punch down) the dough
and turn out on to a lightly floured
surface. Knead lightly and shape into a
ball. Place seam side down and make
a hole in the centre with your fingers.

5 Gradually enlarge the cavity, turning
the dough to make a 25cm/10in circle.
Transfer to the baking sheet, cover with
lightly oiled clear film (plastic wrap) and
leave to rise, in a warm place, for 30–45
minutes, or until doubled in size.

6 Meanwhile, preheat the oven to 200°C/
400°F/Gas 6. Brush the loaf with beaten
egg and sprinkle with poppy seeds. Bake
for 35 minutes, or until golden. Cool on
a wire rack.

BLINIS

*Blinis are the celebrated leavened Russian pancakes. Traditionally served
with sour cream and caviar, they have a very distinctive flavour and
a fluffy, light texture.*

50g/2oz/½ cup buckwheat flour
50g/2oz/½ cup unbleached plain
(all-purpose) flour
2.5ml/½ tsp freshly ground
black pepper
5ml/1 tsp salt
15g/½ oz fresh yeast
200ml/7fl oz/scant 1 cup lukewarm
milk
1 egg, separated

MAKES ABOUT 10 BLINIS

VARIATION
You can use all buckwheat flour,
which will give the blinis a
stronger flavour.

1 Mix the buckwheat flour, plain flour,
pepper and salt together in a large bowl.

2 In a small bowl, cream the yeast with
60ml/4 tbsp of the milk, then mix in the
remaining milk.

3 Add the egg yolk to the flour mixture
and gradually whisk in the yeast mixture
to form a smooth batter. Cover with
clear film (plastic wrap) and leave to
stand in a warm place for 1 hour.

4 Whisk the egg white until it forms soft
peaks and fold into the batter. Lightly oil
a heavy frying pan and heat it.

5 Add about 45ml/3 tbsp of the batter to
make a 10cm/4in round pancake. Cook
until the surface begins to dry out, then
turn the pancake over using a metal
spatula and cook for 1–2 minutes. Repeat
with the remaining batter. Serve warm.

Per loaf Energy 2979kcal/12601kJ; Protein 87.8g; Carbohydrate 547.8g, of which sugars 33.5g; Fat 64.3g, of which saturates 33.4g; Cholesterol 505mg; Calcium 1440mg; Fibre 20.9g; Sodium 4657mg.
Per blini Energy 113kcal/471kJ; Protein 2.7g; Carbohydrate 8g, of which sugars 1.4g; Fat 8g, of which saturates 4.9g; Cholesterol 45mg; Calcium 21mg; Fibre 1g; Sodium 143mg.

POPPY SEED ROLL

350g/12oz/3 cups unbleached white
bread flour
2.5ml/½ tsp salt
25g/1oz/2 tbsp caster (superfine) sugar
20g/¾ oz fresh yeast
120ml/4fl oz/½ cup lukewarm milk
1 egg, lightly beaten
50g/2oz/¼ cup butter, melted
115g/4oz/1 cup icing
(confectioners') sugar
15ml/1 tbsp lemon juice
10–15ml/2–3 tsp water
15ml/1 tbsp toasted flaked
(sliced) almonds

FOR THE FILLING
115g/4oz/⅔ cup poppy seeds
50g/2oz/¼ cup butter
75g/3oz/6 tbsp caster (superfine) sugar
75g/3oz/½ cup raisins
50g/2oz/½ cup ground almonds
50g/2oz/⅓ cup mixed (candied) peel,
finely chopped
2.5ml/½ tsp ground cinnamon

MAKES 1 LARGE LOAF

A favourite sweet yeast bread in both Poland and Hungary, this has an
unusual filling of poppy seeds, almonds, raisins and citrus peel spiralling
through the dough.

1 Lightly grease a baking sheet. Sift the flour and salt together into a large bowl. Stir in the sugar. Cream the yeast with the milk. Add to the flour with the egg and melted butter and mix to a dough.

2 Turn out on to a lightly floured surface and knead for 8–10 minutes until smooth and elastic. Place in a lightly oiled bowl, cover with lightly oiled clear film (plastic wrap) and leave to rise, in a warm place, for 1–1½ hours, or until doubled in size.

3 Meanwhile, pour boiling water over the poppy seeds for the filling, then leave to cool. Drain thoroughly in a fine sieve. Melt the butter in a small pan, add the poppy seeds and cook, stirring, for 1–2 minutes. Remove from the heat and stir in the sugar, raisins, ground almonds, peel and cinnamon. Leave to cool.

4 Turn the dough out on to a lightly floured surface, knock back (punch down) and knead lightly. Roll out into a rectangle 35 × 25cm/14 × 10in. Spread the filling to within 2cm/¾in of the edges.

5 Roll up the dough, starting from one long edge, like a Swiss (jelly) roll, tucking in the edges to seal. Place seam side down on the prepared baking sheet. Cover with lightly oiled clear film and leave to rise, in a warm place, for 30 minutes, or until doubled in size.

6 Meanwhile, preheat the oven to 190°C/375°F/Gas 5. Bake for 30 minutes, or until golden brown. Transfer to a wire rack to cool until just warm.

7 Mix the icing sugar, lemon juice and sufficient water together in a small pan to make an icing stiff enough to coat the back of a spoon. Heat gently, stirring, until warm. Drizzle the icing over the loaf and sprinkle the flaked almonds over the top. Leave to cool completely, then serve sliced.

Per loaf Energy 4341kcal/18218kJ; Protein 91.1g; Carbohydrate 557g, of which sugars 211.5g; Fat 206.1g, of which saturates 69.5g; Cholesterol 426mg; Calcium 1982mg; Fibre 32.8g; Sodium 986mg.

RUSSIAN POTATO BREAD

*In Russia, potatoes are often used to replace some of the flour in bread
recipes. They endow the bread with excellent keeping qualities.*

1 Lightly grease a baking sheet. Add the
potatoes to a pan of boiling water and
cook until tender. Drain and reserve
150ml/¼ pint/⅔ cup of the cooking
water. Mash and sieve the potatoes and
leave to cool.

2 Mix the yeast, bread flours, caraway
seeds and salt together in a large bowl.
Add the butter and rub in. Mix the
reserved potato water and sieved
potatoes together. Gradually work this
mixture into the flour mixture to form a
soft dough.

3 Turn out on to a lightly floured surface
and knead for 8–10 minutes until
smooth and elastic. Place in a lightly
oiled bowl, cover with oiled clear film
(plastic wrap) and leave in a warm place,
for 1 hour, or until doubled in bulk.

4 Turn out on to a lightly floured
surface, knock back (punch down) and
knead gently. Shape into a plump oval
loaf, about 18cm/7in long. Place on the
prepared baking sheet and sprinkle with
a little wholemeal bread flour.

5 Cover the dough with lightly oiled
clear film and leave to rise, in a warm
place, for 30 minutes, or until doubled in
size. Meanwhile, preheat the oven to
200°C/400°F/Gas 6.

6 Using a sharp knife, slash the top with
3–4 diagonal cuts to make a criss-cross
effect. Bake for 30–35 minutes, or until
golden and sounding hollow when
tapped on the base. Transfer to a wire
rack to cool.

*225g/8oz potatoes, peeled
and diced
7g/¼ oz sachet easy bake
(rapid-rise) dried yeast
350g/12oz/3 cups unbleached white
bread flour
115g/4oz/1 cup wholemeal
(whole-wheat) bread flour,
plus extra for sprinkling
2.5ml/½ tsp caraway
seeds, crushed
10ml/2 tsp salt
25g/1oz/2 tbsp butter*

MAKES 1 LOAF

VARIATION
To make a cheese-flavoured potato
bread, omit the caraway seeds and
knead 115g/4oz/1 cup grated Cheddar,
Red Leicester or a crumbled blue
cheese, such as Stilton, into the
dough before shaping.

Per loaf Energy 1893kcal/8026kJ; Protein 51.5g; Carbohydrate 381.8g, of which sugars 10.7g; Fat 28.3g, of which saturates 14.3g; Cholesterol 53mg; Calcium 553mg; Fibre 23.4g; Sodium 4120mg.

KNACKERBRÖD

A very traditional Swedish crispbread with a lovely rye flavour.

450g/1lb/4 cups rye flour
5ml/1 tsp salt
50g/2oz/¼ cup butter
20g/¾ oz fresh yeast
275ml/9fl oz/generous 1 cup
lukewarm water
75g/3oz/2 cups wheat bran

MAKES 8 CRISPBREADS

3 Divide the dough into eight equal pieces and roll each one out on a lightly floured surface, to a 20cm/8in round.

1 Lightly grease two baking sheets. Preheat the oven to 230°C/450°F/Gas 8. Mix the rye flour and salt in a large bowl. Rub in the butter, then make a well in the centre.

2 Cream the yeast with a little water, then stir in the remainder. Pour into the centre of the flour, mix to a dough, then mix in the bran. Knead on a lightly floured surface for 5 minutes until smooth and elastic.

4 Place two rounds on the prepared baking sheets and prick all over with a fork. Cut a hole in the centre of each round, using a 4cm/1½ in cutter.

5 Bake for 15–20 minutes, or until the crispbreads are golden and crisp. Transfer to a wire rack to cool. Repeat with the remaining crispbreads.

COOK'S TIP
The hole in the centre of these crispbreads is a reminder of the days when breads were strung on a pole, which was hung across the rafters to dry. Make smaller crispbreads, if you like, and tie them together with bright red ribbon for an unusual Christmas gift.

FINNISH BARLEY BREAD

In Northern Europe breads are often made using cereals such as barley and rye, which produce very satisfying, tasty breads. This quick-to-prepare flat bread is best served warm with lashings of butter.

225g/8oz/2 cups barley flour
5ml/1 tsp salt
10ml/2 tsp baking powder
25g/1oz/2 tbsp butter, melted
120ml/4fl oz/½ cup single
(light) cream
60ml/4 tbsp milk

MAKES 1 SMALL LOAF

1 Lightly grease a baking sheet. Preheat the oven to 200°C/400°F/Gas 6. Sift the dry ingredients into a bowl. Add the butter, cream and milk. Mix to a dough.

2 Turn out the dough on to a lightly floured surface and shape into a flat round about 1cm/½ in thick.

3 Transfer to the prepared baking sheet and using a sharp knife, lightly mark the top into six sections.

4 Prick the surface of the round evenly with a fork. Bake for 15–18 minutes, or until pale golden. Cut into wedges and serve warm.

COOK'S TIPS
• This flat bread tastes very good with cottage cheese, especially cottage cheese with chives.
• For a citrusy tang, add 10–15ml/ 2–3 tsp finely grated lemon, lime or orange rind to the flour mixture in step 1.

Per crispbread Energy 254kcal/1075kJ; Protein 6g; Carbohydrate 45.2g, of which sugars 0.4g; Fat 6.8g, of which saturates 3.6g; Cholesterol 14mg; Calcium 29mg; Fibre 10g; Sodium 296mg.
Per loaf Energy 1259kcal/5309kJ; Protein 23g; Carbohydrate 196g, of which sugars 7.9g; Fat 48.2g, of which saturates 28.4g; Cholesterol 127mg; Calcium 230mg; Fibre 0g; Sodium 2251mg.

LUSSE BRÖD

120ml/4fl oz/½ cup milk
pinch of saffron threads
400g/14oz/3½ cups unbleached white
bread flour
50g/2oz/½ cup ground almonds
2.5ml/½ tsp salt
75g/3oz/6 tbsp caster (superfine) sugar
25g/1oz fresh yeast
120ml/4fl oz/½ cup lukewarm water
few drops of almond essence (extract)
50g/2oz/¼ cup butter, softened

FOR THE GLAZE
1 egg
15ml/1 tbsp water

MAKES 12 BUNS

VARIATION
Gently knead in 40g/1½ oz/3 tbsp currants after knocking back the dough in step 4.

Saint Lucia Day, the 12th of December, marks the beginning of Christmas in Sweden. As part of the celebrations, young girls dressed in white robes wear headbands topped with lighted candles and walk through the village streets offering saffron buns to the townspeople.

1 Lightly grease two baking sheets. Place the milk in a small pan and bring to the boil. Add the saffron, remove from the heat and leave to infuse (steep) for about 15 minutes. Meanwhile mix the flour, ground almonds, salt and sugar together in a large bowl.

2 Cream the yeast with the water. Add the saffron liquid, yeast mixture and almond essence to the flour mixture and mix to a dough. Gradually beat in the softened butter.

3 Turn out on to a lightly floured surface and knead for 5 minutes until smooth and elastic. Place in a lightly oiled bowl, cover with lightly oiled clear film (plastic wrap) and leave in a warm place, for about 1 hour, or until doubled in bulk.

4 Turn out on to a lightly floured surface and knock back (punch down). Divide into 12 equal pieces and make into different shapes: roll into a long rope and shape into an "S" shape; to make a star, cut a dough piece in half and roll into two ropes, cross one over the other and coil the ends; make an upturned "U" shape and coil the ends to represent curled hair; divide a dough piece in half, roll into two thin ropes and twist together.

5 Place on the prepared baking sheets, spaced well apart, cover with lightly oiled clear film and leave to rise, in a warm place, for about 30 minutes.

6 Meanwhile, preheat the oven to 200°C/400°F/Gas 6. Beat the egg with the water for the glaze, and brush over the rolls. Bake for 15 minutes, or until golden. Transfer to a wire rack to cool slightly to serve warm, or cool completely to serve cold.

Per bun Energy 199kcal/840kJ; Protein 4.4g; Carbohydrate 33.2g, of which sugars 7.7g; Fat 6.3g, of which saturates 2.6g; Cholesterol 10mg; Calcium 73mg; Fibre 1.3g; Sodium 121mg.

VÖRT LIMPA

*This festive Swedish bread is flavoured with warm spices and fresh orange.
The beer and port work nicely to soften the rye taste. The added sugars also
give the yeast a little extra to feed on and so help aerate and lighten the
bread. It is traditionally served with cheese.*

350g/12oz/3 cups rye flour
350g/12oz/3 cups unbleached white
bread flour
2.5ml/½ tsp salt
25g/1oz/2 tbsp caster (superfine) sugar
5ml/1 tsp grated nutmeg
5ml/1 tsp ground cloves
5ml/1 tsp ground ginger
40g/1½ oz fresh yeast
300ml/½ pint/1¼ cups light ale
120ml/4fl oz/½ cup port
15ml/1 tbsp molasses
25g/1oz/2 tbsp butter, melted
15ml/1 tbsp grated orange rind
75g/3oz/½ cup raisins
15ml/1 tbsp malt extract, for glazing

MAKES 1 LARGE LOAF

> **VARIATION**
> This bread can be shaped into a
> round or oval and baked on a baking
> sheet if you prefer.

1 Lightly grease a 30 × 10cm/12 × 4in
loaf tin (pan). Mix together the rye and
white flours, salt, sugar, nutmeg, cloves
and ginger in a large bowl.

2 In another large bowl, using a wooden
spoon, blend the yeast into the ale until
dissolved, then stir in the port, molasses
and melted butter.

3 Gradually add the flour mixture to the
yeast liquid, beating to make a smooth
batter. Continue adding the flour a little
at a time and mixing until the mixture
forms a soft dough.

4 Turn out on to a lightly floured surface
and knead for 8–10 minutes until
smooth and elastic. Place in a lightly
oiled bowl, cover with oiled clear film
(plastic wrap) and leave in a warm
place, for 1 hour, or until doubled in size.

5 Turn out the dough on to a lightly
floured surface and knock back (punch
down). Gently knead in the orange rind
and raisins. Roll into a 30cm/12in square.

6 Fold the bottom third of the dough
up and the top third down, sealing the
edges. Place in the prepared tin, cover
with lightly oiled clear film and leave to
rise, in a warm place, for 1 hour, or until
the dough reaches the top of the tin.

7 Meanwhile, preheat the oven to 190°C/
375°F/Gas 5. Bake for 35–40 minutes, or
until browned. Turn out on to a wire
rack, brush with malt extract and leave
to cool.

Per loaf Energy 3362kcal/14252kJ; Protein 68.8g; Carbohydrate 666.2g, of which sugars 126.8g; Fat 34.9g, of which saturates 15.6g; Cholesterol 58mg; Calcium 812mg; Fibre 53.3g; Sodium 1302mg.

BREADS OF THE AMERICAS

Yeast breads, quick breads based on baking powder, Mexican flat breads and sweet breads are all part of the diverse range found in the Americas. Traditional American ingredients such as corn meal, molasses, sweetcorn and pumpkin provide the distinctive flavours associated with Boston brown bread, corn bread, Virginia spoon bread and pumpkin and walnut bread. San Fransisco sourdough bread gains its unusual flavour not so much from its ingredients but from the fermenting process used in leavening.

SAN FRANCISCO SOURDOUGH BREAD

In San Francisco this bread is leavened using a flour and water paste, which is left to ferment with the aid of airborne yeast. The finished loaves have a moist crumb and crispy crust, and will keep for several days.

FOR THE STARTER
50g/2oz/1/2 cup wholemeal
(whole-wheat) flour
pinch of ground cumin
15ml/1 tbsp milk
15–30ml/1–2 tbsp water
1ST REFRESHMENT
30ml/2 tbsp water
115g/4oz/1 cup wholemeal flour
2ND REFRESHMENT
60ml/4 tbsp water
115g/4oz/1 cup white bread flour

FOR THE BREAD: 1ST REFRESHMENT
75ml/5 tbsp very warm water
75g/3oz/3/4 cup unbleached plain
(all-purpose) flour
2ND REFRESHMENT
175ml/6fl oz/3/4 cup lukewarm water
200–225g/7–8oz/13/4–2 cups
unbleached plain flour

FOR THE SOURDOUGH
280ml/9fl oz/11/4 cups warm water
500g/11/4lb/5 cups unbleached white
bread flour
15ml/1 tbsp salt
flour, for dusting
ice cubes, for baking

MAKES 2 ROUND LOAVES

1 Sift the flour and cumin for the starter into a bowl. Add the milk and sufficient water to make a firm but moist dough. Knead for 6–8 minutes to form a firm dough. Return the dough to the bowl, cover with a damp dishtowel and leave in a warm place, 24–26°C/75–80°F, for about 2 days. When it is ready the starter will appear moist and wrinkled and will have developed a crust.

2 Pull off the hardened crust and discard. Scoop out the moist centre (about the size of a hazelnut), which will be aerated and sweet smelling, and place in a clean bowl. Mix in the water for the 1st refreshment. Gradually add the wholemeal flour and mix to a dough.

3 Cover with clear film (plastic wrap) and return to a warm place for 1–2 days. Discard the crust and gradually mix in the water for the 2nd refreshment to the starter, which by now will have a slightly sharper smell. Gradually mix in the white flour, cover and leave in a warm place for 8–10 hours.

4 For the bread, mix the sourdough starter with the water for the 1st refreshment. Gradually mix in the flour to form a firm dough. Knead for 6–8 minutes until firm. Cover with a damp dishtowel and leave in a warm place for 8–12 hours, or until doubled in bulk.

5 Gradually mix in the water for the 2nd refreshment, then gradually mix in enough flour to form a soft, smooth elastic dough. Re-cover and leave in a warm place for 8–12 hours. Gradually stir in the water for the sourdough, then gradually work in the flour and salt. This will take 10–15 minutes. Turn out on to a lightly floured surface and knead until smooth and very elastic. Place in a large lightly oiled bowl, cover with lightly oiled clear film and leave to rise, in a warm place, for 8–12 hours.

6 Divide the dough in half and shape into two round loaves by folding the sides over to the centre and sealing.

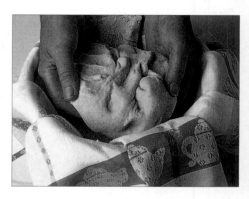

7 Place seam side up in flour-dusted *couronnes*, bowls or baskets lined with flour-dusted dish towels. Re-cover and leave to rise in a warm place for 4 hours.

8 Preheat the oven to 220°C/425°F/ Gas 7. Place an empty roasting pan in the bottom of the oven. Dust two baking sheets with flour. Turn out the loaves seam side down on the prepared baking sheets. Using a sharp knife, cut a criss-cross pattern by slashing the top of the loaves four or five times in each direction.

9 Place the baking sheets in the oven and immediately drop the ice cubes into the hot roasting pan to create steam. Bake the bread for 25 minutes, then reduce the oven temperature to 200°C/ 400°F/Gas 6 and bake for a further 15–20 minutes, or until sounding hollow when tapped on the base. Transfer to wire racks to cool.

COOK'S TIP
If you'd like to make sourdough bread regularly, keep a small amount of the starter covered in the refrigerator. It will keep for several days. Use the starter for the 2nd refreshment, then continue as directed.

Per loaf Energy 1749kcal/7435kJ; Protein 48.2g; Carbohydrate 398.4g, of which sugars 7.7g; Fat 6.7g, of which saturates 1.1g; Cholesterol 0mg; Calcium 718mg; Fibre 15.9g; Sodium 1490mg.

BOSTON BROWN BREAD

90g/3¹/2 oz/scant 1 cup corn meal
90g/3¹/2 oz/scant 1 cup unbleached
plain (all-purpose) white flour or
wholemeal (whole-wheat) flour
90g/3¹/2 oz/scant 1 cup rye flour
2.5ml/¹/2 tsp salt
5ml/1 tsp bicarbonate of soda
(baking soda)
90g/3¹/2 oz/generous ¹/2 cup raisins
120ml/4fl oz/¹/2 cup milk
120ml/4fl oz/¹/2 cup water
120ml/4fl oz/¹/2 cup molasses

MAKES 1 OR 2 LOAVES

Rich, moist and dark, this bread is flavoured with molasses and can include raisins. In Boston it is often served with savoury baked beans.

COOK'S TIP
If you do not have empty coffee jugs, cans or similar moulds, cook the bread in one or two heatproof bowls of equivalent capacity.

1 Line the base of one 1.2 litre/2 pint/ 5 cup cylindrical metal or glass container, such as a heatproof glass coffee jug (carafe), with greased greaseproof (waxed) paper. Alternatively, remove the lids from two 450g/1lb coffee cans, wash and dry them thoroughly, then line with greased greaseproof paper.

2 Mix together the corn meal, plain or wholemeal flour, rye flour, salt, bicarbonate of soda and raisins in a large bowl. Warm the milk and water in a small pan and stir in the molasses.

3 Add the molasses mixture to the dry ingredients and mix together using a spoon until it just forms a moist dough. Do not overmix.

4 Fill the jug or cans with the dough; they should be about two-thirds full. Cover neatly with foil or greased greaseproof paper and tie securely.

5 Bring water to a depth of 5cm/2in to the boil in a deep, heavy pan large enough to accommodate the jug or cans. Place a trivet in the pan, stand the jug or cans on top, cover the pan and steam for 1¹/2 hours, adding more boiling water to maintain the required level as necessary.

6 Cool the loaves for a few minutes in the jug or cans, then turn them on their sides and the loaves should slip out. Serve warm, as a teabread or with savoury dishes.

Per loaf Energy 774kcal/3285kJ; Protein 15.8g; Carbohydrate 176.5g, of which sugars 75.2g; Fat 4.2g, of which saturates 0.8g; Cholesterol 4mg; Calcium 472mg; Fibre 8.6g; Sodium 611mg.

PUMPKIN AND WALNUT BREAD

Pumpkin, nutmeg and walnuts combine to yield a moist, tangy and slightly sweet bread with an indescribably good flavour. Serve partnered with meats or cheese, or simply lightly buttered.

1 Grease and neatly base line a loaf tin (pan) measuring 21.5 × 11cm/8½ × 4½in. Preheat the oven to 180°C/350°F/Gas 4.

2 Place the pumpkin in a pan, add water to cover by about 5cm/2in, then bring to the boil. Cover, lower the heat and simmer for 20 minutes, or until the pumpkin is very tender. Drain well, then purée in a food processor or blender. Leave to cool.

3 Place 275g/10oz/1¼ cups of the purée in a large bowl. Add the sugar, nutmeg, melted butter and eggs to the purée and mix together. Sift the flour, baking powder and salt together into a large bowl and make a well in the centre.

4 Add the pumpkin mixture to the centre of the flour and stir until smooth. Mix in the walnuts.

500g/1¼ lb pumpkin, peeled, seeded
and cut into chunks
75g/3oz/6 tbsp caster
(superfine) sugar
5ml/1 tsp grated nutmeg
50g/2oz/¼ cup butter, melted
3 eggs, lightly beaten
350g/12oz/3 cups unbleached white
bread flour
10ml/2 tsp baking powder
2.5ml/½ tsp salt
75g/3oz/¾ cup walnuts, chopped

MAKES 1 LOAF

COOK'S TIP
You may have slightly more pumpkin purée than you actually need – use the remainder in soup.

5 Transfer to the prepared tin and bake for 1 hour, or until golden and starting to shrink from the sides of the tin. Turn out on to a wire rack to cool.

Per loaf Energy 2663kcal/11186kJ; Protein 66.8g; Carbohydrate 364.1g, of which sugars 94.4g; Fat 114.7g, of which saturates 36.1g; Cholesterol 677mg; Calcium 840mg; Fibre 18.5g; Sodium 1516mg.

*225g/8oz/2 cups unbleached plain
(all-purpose) flour
5ml/1 tsp salt
4ml/³/4 tsp baking powder
40g/1¹/2 oz/3 tbsp lard (shortening)
or vegetable fat
150ml/¹/4 pint/²/3 cup warm water*

MAKES 12 TORTILLAS

COOK'S TIPS
• Tortillas are delicious either as an accompaniment or filled with roast chicken or cooked minced (ground) meat, refried beans and/or salad to serve as a snack or light lunch.
• To reheat tortillas, wrap in foil and warm in a moderate oven, 180°C/350°F/Gas 4, for about 5 minutes.

*75g/3oz/³/4 cup unbleached white
bread flour
150g/6oz/1¹/2 cups yellow corn meal
5ml/1 tsp salt
25ml/1¹/2 tbsp baking powder
15ml/1 tbsp caster (superfine) sugar
50g/2oz/4 tbsp butter, melted
250ml/8fl oz/1 cup milk
3 eggs
200g/7oz/scant 1¹/4 cups canned corn,
drained*

MAKES 1 LARGE LOAF

VARIATIONS
• Bake this corn bread in a 20cm/8in square cake tin (pan) instead of a round one if you wish to cut it into squares or rectangles.
• If you would prefer a more rustic corn bread, replace some or all of the white bread flour with wholemeal (whole-wheat) bread flour.

WHEAT TORTILLAS

Tortillas are the staple flat bread in Mexico, where they are often made from masa harina, a flour milled from corn. These soft wheat tortillas are also popular in the South-western states of the USA.

1 Mix the flour, salt and baking powder in a bowl. Rub in the fat, stir in the water and knead lightly to a soft dough. Cover with clear film (plastic wrap) and leave to rest for 15 minutes. Divide into 12 pieces and shape into balls. Roll out on a floured surface into 15–18cm/ 6–7in rounds. Re-cover to keep moist.

2 Heat a heavy frying pan or griddle, add one tortilla and cook for 1¹/2–2 minutes, turning over as soon as the surface starts to bubble. It should stay flexible. Remove from the pan and wrap in a dishtowel to keep warm while cooking the remaining tortillas in the same way.

DOUBLE CORN BREAD

In the American South, corn bread is made with white corn meal and is fairly flat, while in the North it is thicker and made with yellow corn meal. Whatever the version it's delicious – this recipe combines yellow corn meal with sweetcorn. It is marvellous served warm, cut into wedges and buttered.

1 Preheat the oven to 200°C/400°F/ Gas 6. Grease and base line a 22cm/ 8¹/2 in round cake tin (pan). Sift the flour, corn meal, salt and baking powder together into a large bowl. Stir in the sugar and make a well in the centre.

3 Using a wooden spoon, stir the canned corn quickly into the mixture. Pour into the prepared tin and bake for 20–25 minutes, or until a metal skewer inserted into the centre comes out clean.

2 Mix the melted butter, milk and eggs together. Add to the centre of the flour mixture and beat until just combined.

4 Invert the bread on to a wire rack and lift off the lining paper. Cool slightly. Serve warm, cut into wedges.

Per tortilla Energy 94kcal/394kJ; Protein 1.8g; Carbohydrate 14.6g, of which sugars 0.3g; Fat 3.5g, of which saturates 1.4g; Cholesterol 3mg; Calcium 26mg; Fibre 0.6g; Sodium 164mg.
Per loaf Energy 1818kcal/7623kJ; Protein 54.6g; Carbohydrate 248.9g, of which sugars 48.1g; Fat 70.3g, of which saturates 33.9g; Cholesterol 692mg; Calcium 520mg; Fibre 8.4g; Sodium 1164mg.

VIRGINIA SPOON BREAD

Spoon bread is a traditional dish from the southern states of America, which, according to legend, originated when too much water was added to a corn bread batter and the baked bread had to be spooned out of the tin. Served hot from the oven, this ethereally light offering – enhanced with Cheddar cheese and a hint of garlic – is delicious.

450ml/³/4 pint/1³/4 cups milk
75g/3oz/²/3 cup corn meal
15g/¹/2 oz/1 tbsp butter
75g/3oz/³/4 cup grated mature
(sharp) Cheddar cheese
1 garlic clove
3 eggs, separated
75g/3oz/¹/2 cup corn
kernels (optional)
salt and freshly ground black pepper

MAKES 1 LARGE LOAF

VARIATIONS
Add 115g/4oz fried chopped bacon or 5–10ml/1–2 tsp finely chopped green chilli for different flavoured spoon breads.

1 Preheat the oven to 180°C/350°F/ Gas 4. Grease a 1.5 litre/2¹/2 pint/6 cup soufflé dish.

2 Place the milk in a large heavy pan. Heat gently, then gradually add the corn meal, stirring. Add salt and slowly bring to the boil, stirring all the time. Cook for 5–10 minutes, stirring frequently, until thick and smooth.

3 Remove from the heat and stir in the butter, Cheddar cheese, garlic and egg yolks. Season to taste.

4 In a bowl, whisk the egg whites until they form soft peaks. Stir one-quarter into the corn meal mixture and then gently fold in the remainder. Fold in the well-drained corn, if using.

5 Spoon the mixture into the prepared soufflé dish and bake for 45–50 minutes, or until puffed and beginning to brown. Serve at once.

COOK'S TIPS
• Use a perfectly clean bowl and whisk for whisking the egg whites and make sure it is free of grease by washing and drying thoroughly, then wiping out with a little lemon juice.
• If any shell drops in with the egg, scoop it out with another, larger piece of shell.

Per loaf Energy 1126kcal/4699kJ; Protein 59.8g; Carbohydrate 77.4g, of which sugars 22.6g; Fat 63.6g, of which saturates 33.5g; Cholesterol 705mg; Calcium 1184mg; Fibre 1.6g; Sodium 1112mg.

NEW ENGLAND FANTANS

These fantail rolls look stylish and are so versatile that they are equally suitable for a simple snack, or a gourmet dinner party!

1 Grease a muffin sheet with 9 × 7.5cm/ 3in cups or foil cases. Mix the yeast with the buttermilk and sugar and then leave to stand for 15 minutes.

2 In a pan, heat the milk with 40g/1½oz/ 3 tbsp of the butter until the butter has melted. Cool until lukewarm.

3 Sift the flour and salt together into a large bowl. Add the yeast mixture, milk mixture and egg and mix to a soft dough. Turn out on to a lightly floured surface and knead for 5–8 minutes until smooth and elastic. Place in a lightly oiled bowl, cover with oiled clear film (plastic wrap) and leave in a warm place, for about 1 hour, until doubled in size.

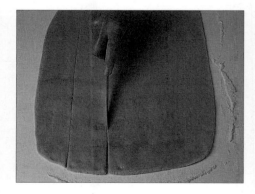

4 Turn out on to a lightly floured surface, knock back (punch down) and knead until smooth and elastic. Roll into an oblong measuring 45 × 30cm/18 × 12in and about 5mm/¼ in thick. Melt the remaining butter, brush over the dough and cut it lengthways into five equal strips. Stack on top of each other and cut across into nine equal 5cm/2in strips.

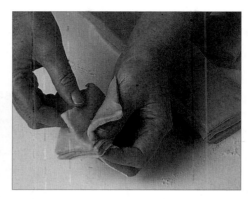

5 Pinch one side of each layered strip together, then place pinched side down into a prepared muffin cup or foil case. Cover with lightly oiled clear film and leave to rise, in a warm place, for 30–40 minutes, or until the fantans have almost doubled in size. Meanwhile, preheat the oven to 200°C/400°F/Gas 6. Bake for 20 minutes, or until golden. Turn out on to a wire rack to cool.

15g/½ oz fresh yeast
75ml/5 tbsp buttermilk, at room temperature
10ml/2 tsp caster (superfine) sugar
75ml/5 tbsp milk
65g/2½ oz/5 tbsp butter
375g/13oz/3¼ cups unbleached white bread flour
5ml/1 tsp salt
1 egg, lightly beaten

MAKES 9 ROLLS

VARIATION
To make Cinnamon-spiced Fantans, add 5ml/1 tsp ground cinnamon to the remaining butter in step 4 before brushing over the dough strips. Sprinkle the rolls with a little icing (confectioners') sugar as soon as they come out of the oven, then leave to cool before serving.

Per roll Energy 215kcal/905kJ; Protein 5.2g; Carbohydrate 34.4g, of which sugars 2.6g; Fat 7.2g, of which saturates 4.3g; Cholesterol 39mg; Calcium 83mg; Fibre 1.3g; Sodium 291mg.

MEXICAN "BREAD OF THE DEAD"

A celebratory loaf made for All Souls' Day. Even though the name of this bread suggests otherwise, it is actually a very happy day when both Mexicans and Spanish people pay their respects to the souls of their dead. Traditionally the bread is decorated with a dough skull, bones and tears.

3 star anise
90ml/6 tbsp cold water
675g/1 1/2 lb/6 cups unbleached white bread flour
5ml/1 tsp salt
115g/4oz/1/2 cup caster (superfine) sugar
25g/1oz fresh yeast
175ml/6fl oz/3/4 cup lukewarm water
3 eggs
60ml/4 tbsp orange liqueur
115g/4oz/1/2 cup butter, melted
grated rind of 1 orange
icing (confectioners') sugar, for dusting

MAKES 1 LARGE LOAF

VARIATION
Top the baked bread with orange icing. Blend 60g/2oz/1/2 cup icing sugar and 15–30ml/1–2 tbsp orange liqueur. Pour the icing over the bread and let it dribble down the sides.

1 Grease a 26cm/10 1/2 in fluted round cake tin (pan). Place the star anise in a small pan and add the cold water. Bring to the boil and boil for 3–4 minutes, or until the liquid has reduced to 45ml/3 tbsp. Discard the star anise and leave the liquid to cool.

2 Sift the flour and salt together into a large bowl. Stir in the sugar and make a well in the centre.

3 In a jug (pitcher), dissolve the yeast in the lukewarm water. Pour into the centre of the flour and mix in a little flour, using your fingers, until a smooth, thick batter forms. Sprinkle over a little of the remaining flour, cover with clear film(plastic wrap) and leave the batter in a warm place for 30 minutes, or until the mixture starts to bubble.

4 Beat the eggs, the reserved liquid flavoured with star anise, orange liqueur and melted butter together. Gradually incorporate into the flour mixture to form a smooth dough.

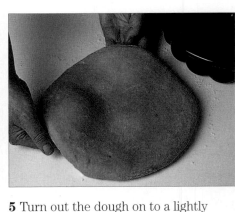

5 Turn out the dough on to a lightly floured surface and gently knead in the orange rind. Knead for 5–6 minutes until smooth and elastic. Shape into a 26cm/10 1/2 in round and place in the prepared tin. Cover with lightly oiled clear film and leave to rise, in a warm place, for 2–3 hours, or until almost at the top of the tin and doubled in bulk.

6 Meanwhile, preheat the oven to 190°C/375°F/Gas 5. Bake the loaf for 45–50 minutes, or until golden. Turn out on to a wire rack to cool. Dust with icing sugar to serve.

Per loaf Energy 3617kcal/15231kJ; Protein 82.8g; Carbohydrate 554.8g, of which sugars 40.4g; Fat 119.4g, of which saturates 68.1g; Cholesterol 835mg; Calcium 1056mg; Fibre 20.9g; Sodium 3062mg.

WEST INDIAN ROTIS

Caribbean food is based on cuisines from many areas of the world, influenced by a wide range of cultures. It is the Anglo-Indian connection that brought the Indian flatbread called roti to Trinidad in the West Indies.

450g/1lb/4 cups atta *or fine wholemeal (whole-wheat) flour*
5ml/1 tsp baking powder
5ml/1 tsp salt
300ml/½ pint/1¼ cups water
115–150g/4–5oz/8–10 tbsp clarified butter or ghee

MAKES 8 ROTIS

1 Mix the flour, baking powder and salt together in a large bowl, and make a well in the centre. Gradually mix in the water to make a firm dough.

2 Knead on a lightly floured surface until smooth. Place in a lightly oiled bowl; cover with oiled clear film (plastic wrap). Leave to stand for 20 minutes.

3 Divide the dough into eight equal pieces and roll each one on a lightly floured surface into an 18cm/7in round. Brush the surface of each round with a little of the clarified butter or ghee, fold in half and half again. Cover the folded rounds with lightly oiled clear film and leave for 10 minutes.

4 Take one roti and roll out on a lightly floured surface into a round about 20–23cm/8–9in in diameter. Brush both sides with some clarified butter or ghee.

5 Heat a griddle or heavy frying pan, add the roti and cook for about 1 minute. Turn over and cook for 2 minutes, then turn over again and cook for 1 minute. Wrap in a dishtowel to keep warm while cooking the remaining rotis. Serve warm.

Per roti Energy 280kcal/1177kJ; Protein 7.2g; Carbohydrate 36g, of which sugars 1.2g; Fat 13g, of which saturates 7.9g; Cholesterol 33mg; Calcium 24mg; Fibre 5.1g; Sodium 355mg.

BREADS OF INDIA AND THE MIDDLE EAST

Chapatis, pooris, rotis and naan are typical unleavened Indian flatbreads. Chillies, herbs and spices are popular additions and cooking methods range from baking in a traditional clay tandoor to frying in oil. The tradition of baking flatbreads continues into the Middle East, although their specialities – crisp lavash, onion breads and barbari – include yeast. All these breads are perfect for serving with soups or dips.

NAAN

From the Caucasus through the Punjab region of northwest India and beyond, all serve these leavened breads. Traditionally cooked in a very hot clay oven known as a tandoor, naan are usually eaten with dry meat or vegetable dishes, such as tandoori.

225g/8oz/2 cups unbleached white bread flour
2.5ml/1/2 tsp salt
15g/1/2 oz fresh yeast
60ml/4 tbsp lukewarm milk
15ml/1 tbsp vegetable oil
30ml/2 tbsp natural (plain) yogurt
1 egg
30–45ml/2–3 tbsp melted ghee or butter, for brushing

MAKES 3 NAAN

1 Sift the flour and salt together into a large bowl. In a smaller bowl, cream the yeast with the milk. Set aside for 15 minutes.

2 Add the yeast mixture, oil, yogurt and egg to the flour and mix to a soft dough.

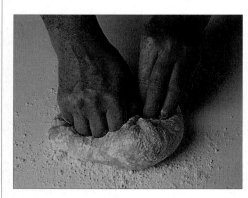

3 Turn out the dough on to a lightly floured surface and knead for about 10 minutes until smooth and elastic. Place in a lightly oiled bowl, cover with lightly oiled clear film (plastic wrap) and leave to rise, in a warm place, for 45 minutes, or until doubled in bulk.

4 Preheat the oven to its highest setting, at least 230°C/450°F/Gas 8. Place three heavy baking sheets in the oven to heat.

5 Turn the dough out on to a lightly floured surface and knock back (punch down). Divide into three and shape into balls.

6 Cover two of the balls of dough with oiled clear film and roll out the third into a teardrop shape about 25cm/10in long, 13cm/5in wide and with a thickness of about 5mm–8mm/1/4–1/3in.

7 Preheat the grill (broiler) to its highest setting. Meanwhile, place the naan on the hot baking sheets and bake for 3–4 minutes, or until puffed up.

8 Remove the naan from the oven and place under the hot grill for a few seconds, or until the top of the naan browns slightly. Wrap the cooked naan in a dishtowel to keep warm while rolling out and cooking the remaining naan. Brush with melted ghee or butter and serve warm.

VARIATIONS
You can flavour naan in numerous different ways:
• To make spicy naan, add 5ml/1 tsp each ground coriander and ground cumin to the flour in step 1. If you would like the naan to be extra fiery, add 2.5–5ml/1/2–1 tsp hot chilli powder.
• To make cardamom-flavoured naan, lightly crush the seeds from 4–5 green cardamom pods and add to the flour in step 1.
• To make poppy seed naan, brush the rolled-out naan with a little ghee and sprinkle with poppy seeds. Press lightly to make sure that they stick.
• To make peppered naan, brush the rolled-out naan with a little ghee and dust generously with coarsely ground black pepper.
• To make onion-flavoured naan, add 114g/4oz/1/2 cup finely chopped or coarsely grated onion to the dough in step 2. You may need to reduce the amount of egg if the onion is very moist to prevent making the dough too soft.
• To make wholemeal naan, substitute wholemeal (whole-wheat) bread flour for some or all of the white flour.

COOK'S TIP
To help the naan dough to puff up and brown, place the baking sheets in an oven preheated to the maximum temperature for at least 10 minutes before baking to ensure that they are hot. Preheat the grill while the naan are baking.

Per naan Energy 315kcal/1334kJ; Protein 9.4g; Carbohydrate 58.5g, of which sugars 1.5g; Fat 6.5g, of which saturates 1.1g; Cholesterol 63mg; Calcium 123mg; Fibre 2.3g; Sodium 356mg.

*115g/4oz/1 cup unbleached plain
(all-purpose) flour
115g/4oz/1 cup wholemeal (whole-
wheat) flour
2.5ml/1/2 tsp salt
2.5ml/1/2 tsp chilli powder (optional)
30ml/2 tbsp vegetable oil
100–120ml/31/2–4fl oz/
scant 1/2 cup water
oil, for frying*

MAKES 12 POORIS

VARIATION
To make spinach-flavoured pooris,
thaw 50g/2oz frozen chopped spinach,
drain it well and add it to the dough
with a little grated fresh root ginger
and 2.5ml/1/2 tsp ground cumin.

175g/6oz/11/2 cups atta *or wholemeal
(whole-wheat) flour
2.5ml/1/2 tsp salt
100–120ml/scant 4fl oz/
scant 1/2 cup water
5ml/1 tsp vegetable oil
melted ghee or butter, for brushing
(optional)*

MAKES 6 CHAPATIS

COOK'S TIP
Atta or *ata* is a very fine wholemeal
flour, which is only found in Indian
stores and supermarkets. It is
sometimes simply labelled chapati
flour. *Atta* can also be used for making
rotis and other Indian flatbreads.

POORIS

*Pooris are small discs of dough that, when fried, puff up into light airy
breads. They will melt in your mouth!*

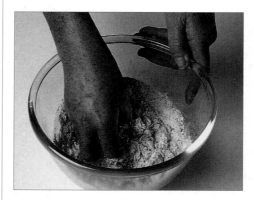

1 Sift the flours, salt and chilli powder,
if using, into a large bowl. Add the
vegetable oil then add sufficient water
to mix to a dough. Turn out on to a
lightly floured surface and knead for
8–10 minutes until smooth.

2 Place in a lightly oiled bowl and cover
with lightly oiled clear film (plastic
wrap). Leave to rest for 30 minutes.

3 Turn out on to a lightly floured
surface. Divide the dough into 12 equal
pieces. Keeping the rest of the dough
covered, roll one piece into a 13cm/5in
round. Repeat with the remaining
dough. Stack the pooris, layered
between clear film, to keep moist.

4 Heat oil to a depth of 2.5cm/1in in a
deep frying pan to 180°C/350°F. Using
a fish slice (metal spatula), lift one poori
and gently slide it into the oil; it will sink
but return to the surface and begin to
sizzle. Gently press the poori into the
oil. It will puff up. Turn over after a few
seconds and cook for 20–30 seconds.

5 Remove the poori from the pan and
drain on kitchen paper. Keep warm in a
low oven while cooking the remaining
pooris. Serve warm.

CHAPATIS

*These chewy, unleavened breads are eaten throughout Northern India. They
are usually served as an accompaniment to spicy dishes.*

2 Knead for 5–6 minutes until smooth.
Place in a lightly oiled bowl, cover with a
damp dishtowel and leave to rest for
30 minutes. Turn out on to a floured
surface. Divide the dough into six equal
pieces. Shape each piece into a ball.

4 Heat a griddle or heavy frying pan
over a medium heat for a few minutes
until hot. Take one chapati, brush off
any excess flour, and place on the
griddle. Cook for 30–60 seconds, or
until the top begins to bubble and white
specks appear on the underside.

5 Turn the chapati over using a metal
spatula and cook for a further 30 seconds.
Remove from the pan and keep warm,
layered between a folded dishtowel,
while cooking the remaining chapatis.
If you like, the chapatis can be brushed
lightly with melted ghee or butter
immediately after cooking. Serve warm.

1 Sift the flour and salt into a bowl. Add
the water and mix to a soft dough.
Knead in the oil, then turn out on to a
lightly floured surface.

3 Press the dough into a larger round
with your palm, then roll into a 13cm/5in
round. Stack, layered between clear film
(plastic wrap), to keep moist.

Per poori Energy 120kcal/501kJ; Protein 2.1g; Carbohydrate 13.5g, of which sugars 0.3g; Fat 6.7g, of which saturates 0.8g; Cholesterol 0mg; Calcium 17mg; Fibre 1.2g; Sodium 164mg.
Per chapati Energy 99kcal/421kJ; Protein 3.7g; Carbohydrate 19.9g, of which sugars 0.5g; Fat 1.1g, of which saturates 0.2g; Cholesterol 0mg; Calcium 38mg; Fibre 1.9g; Sodium 165mg.

MISSI ROTIS

These unleavened breads are a speciality from Punjab in India.
Gram flour, known as besan, is made from chickpeas and is combined here
with the more traditional wheat flour.

115g/4oz/1 cup gram flour
115g/4oz/1 cup wholemeal
(whole-wheat) flour
1 green chilli, seeded and chopped
1/2 onion, finely chopped
15ml/1 tbsp fresh
coriander (cilantro)
2.5ml/1/2 tsp ground turmeric
2.5ml/1/2 tsp salt
15ml/1 tbsp oil or melted butter
120–150ml/4–5fl oz/1/2–2/3 cup
lukewarm water
30–45ml/2–3 tbsp ghee

MAKES 4 ROTIS

VARIATION
Use 1.25–2.5ml/1/4–1/2 tsp chilli
powder in place of the fresh chilli.

1 Chop the coriander and mix with the flours, chilli, onion, turmeric and salt together in a large bowl. Stir in the 15ml/1 tbsp oil or melted butter.

2 Mix in sufficient water to make a pliable soft dough. Turn out the dough on to a lightly floured surface and knead until smooth.

3 Place in a lightly oiled bowl, cover with lightly oiled clear film (plastic wrap) and leave to rest for 1 hour.

4 Turn the dough out on to a lightly floured surface. Divide into four equal pieces and shape into balls. Roll out each ball into a thick round 15–18cm/ 6–7in in diameter.

5 Heat a griddle or heavy frying pan over a medium heat for a few minutes until hot.

6 Brush both sides of one roti with the ghee. Add it to the griddle or frying pan and cook for about 2 minutes, turning after 1 minute. Brush the cooked roti lightly with melted butter or ghee again, slide it on to a plate and keep warm in a low oven while cooking the remaining rotis in the same way. Serve the rotis while still warm.

Per roti Energy 298kcal/1267kJ; Protein 8.5g; Carbohydrate 65.8g, of which sugars 1.6g; Fat 2g, of which saturates 0.3g; Cholesterol 0mg; Calcium 114mg; Fibre 3.2g; Sodium 3mg.

LAVASH

Thin and crispy, this flatbread is universally eaten throughout the Middle East. It's ideal for serving with soups and appetizers, and can be made in any size and broken into pieces as desired.

275g/10oz/2½ cups unbleached white
bread flour
175g/6oz/1½ cups wholemeal
(whole-wheat) flour
5ml/1 tsp salt
15g/½ oz fresh yeast
250ml/8fl oz/1 cup lukewarm water
60ml/4 tbsp natural (plain) yogurt
or milk

MAKES 10 LAVASH

1 Sift the white and wholemeal flours and salt together into a large bowl and make a well in the centre. Mix the yeast with half the lukewarm water until creamy, then stir in the remaining water.

4 Roll the dough as thinly as possible, then lift it over the backs of your hands and gently stretch and turn the dough. Let rest in between rolling for a few minutes if necessary to avoid tearing.

5 As soon as they are ready, place four lavash on the baking sheets and bake for 6–8 minutes, or until starting to brown. Stack the remaining uncooked lavash, layered between clear film or baking parchment, and cover, to keep moist. Transfer to a wire rack to cool and cook the remaining lavash.

2 Add the yeast mixture and yogurt or milk to the centre of the flour and mix to a soft dough. Turn out on to a lightly floured surface and knead for 8–10 minutes until smooth and elastic. Place in a lightly oiled bowl, cover with lightly oiled clear film (plastic wrap) and leave in a warm place, for about 1 hour, or until doubled in bulk. Knock back (punch down), re-cover with lightly oiled clear film and leave to rise for 30 minutes.

3 Turn the dough back out on to a lightly floured surface. Knock back gently and divide into 10 equal pieces. Shape into balls, then flatten into discs with the palm of your hand. Cover and leave to rest for 5 minutes. Meanwhile, preheat the oven to the maximum temperature – at least 230°C/450°F/ Gas 8. Place three or four baking sheets in the oven to heat.

Per lavash Energy 151kcal/644kJ; Protein 5.1g; Carbohydrate 33g, of which sugars 1.2g; Fat 0.8g, of which saturates 0.1g; Cholesterol 0mg; Calcium 57mg; Fibre 2.4g; Sodium 203mg.

Syrian Onion Bread

*450g/1lb/4 cups unbleached white
bread flour
5ml/1 tsp salt
20g/³⁄₄oz fresh yeast
280ml/9fl oz/scant 1¹⁄₄ cups
lukewarm water*

*For the Topping
60ml/4 tbsp finely chopped onion
5ml/1 tsp ground cumin
10ml/2 tsp ground coriander
10ml/2 tsp chopped fresh mint
30ml/2 tbsp olive oil*

Makes 8 Breads

*The basic Arab breads of the Levant and Gulf have traditionally been made
with a finely ground wholemeal flour similar to chapati flour, but now are
being made with white flour as well. This Syrian version has a tasty,
aromatic topping.*

COOK'S TIP
If you haven't any fresh mint to hand,
then add 15ml/1 tbsp dried mint. Use
the freeze-dried variety if you can as
it has much more flavour.

1 Lightly flour two baking sheets. Sift
the flour and salt together into a large
bowl and make a well in the centre.
Cream the yeast with a little of the
water, then mix in the remainder.

2 Add the yeast mixture to the centre of
the flour and mix to a firm dough. Turn
out on to a lightly floured surface and
knead for 8–10 minutes until smooth
and elastic.

3 Place in a lightly oiled bowl, cover
with lightly oiled clear film (plastic
wrap) and leave in a warm place, for
about 1 hour, or until doubled in size.

4 Knock back (punch down) the dough
and turn out on to a lightly floured
surface. Divide into eight equal pieces
and roll into 13–15cm/5–6in rounds.
Make them slightly concave. Prick all
over and space well apart on the baking
sheets. Cover with lightly oiled clear film
and leave to rise for 15–20 minutes.

5 Meanwhile, preheat the oven to 200°C/
400°F/Gas 6. Mix the chopped onion,
ground cumin, ground coriander and
chopped mint in a bowl. Brush the
breads with the olive oil for the topping,
sprinkle them evenly with the spicy
onion mixture and bake for 15–20
minutes. Serve the onion breads warm.

Per bread Energy 220kcal/932kJ; Protein 5.5g; Carbohydrate 44.4g, of which sugars 1.3g; Fat 3.5g, of which saturates 0.5g; Cholesterol 0mg; Calcium 85mg; Fibre 1.9g; Sodium 248mg.

BARBARI

*These small Iranian flatbreads can be made in a variety of sizes. For a
change, make two large breads and break off pieces to scoop up dips.*

1 Lightly dust two baking sheets with
flour. Sift the flour and salt together into
a bowl and make a well in the centre.

2 Mix the yeast with the water. Pour
into the centre of the flour, sprinkle a
little flour over and leave in a warm
place for 15 minutes. Mix to a dough,
then turn out on to a lightly floured
surface and knead for 8–10 minutes
until smooth and elastic.

3 Place in a lightly oiled bowl, cover
with oiled clear film (plastic wrap) and
leave for 45–60 minutes, or until doubled.

4 Knock back (punch down) the dough
and turn out on to a lightly floured
surface. Divide into six equal pieces and
shape into rectangles. Roll each one out
to about 10 × 5cm/4 × 2in and about 1cm/
½in thick. Space well apart on the baking
sheets, and make four slashes in the tops.

*225g/8oz/2 cups unbleached white
bread flour
5ml/1 tsp salt
15g/½oz fresh yeast
140ml/scant ¼ pint/scant ⅔ cup
lukewarm water
oil, for brushing*

MAKES 6 BARBARI

VARIATION
Sprinkle with sesame or caraway
seeds before baking.

5 Cover the breads with lightly oiled
clear film and leave to rise, in a warm
place, for 20 minutes. Meanwhile,
preheat the oven to 200°C/400°F/Gas 6.
Brush the breads with oil and bake for
12–15 minutes, or until pale golden.
Serve warm.

Per barbari Energy 128kcal/544kJ; Protein 3.5g; Carbohydrate 29.1g, of which sugars 0.6g; Fat 0.5g, of which saturates 0.1g; Cholesterol 0mg; Calcium 53mg; Fibre 1.2g; Sodium 329mg.

INDEX

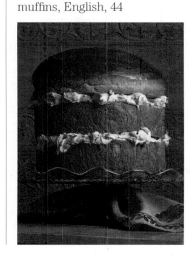

PUBLISHER'S ACKNOWLEDGEMENTS

All recipe pictures and chapter openers are by
Nicki Dowey. The pictures on pages 6–31 are
by Amanda Heywood, except for the following
that have been reproduced with the kind
permission of those listed:
p. 6t, p. 7t, and p. 8b Maison Blanc Limited;
p. 7b Jan Suttle/Life File.